Advance praise

for

UNFREEZING TRAUMA

"Mary J. Held's book, *Unfreezing Trauma,* is a powerful re-living both of her trauma and her healing. At times almost unbearably painful to read, it is nonetheless profoundly hopeful. Mary's courage and integrity in sharing her experience with EMDR Therapy welcome us back to living our lives fully."
Rachel Diem, trauma survivor

"*Unfreezing Trauma* by Mary Held is an amazing and powerful journey of a brave woman who experienced complex trauma. It has the unique perspectives of the Eye Movement Desensitization Reprocessing (EMDR) Therapist and the person's experiences in the same narrative. *Unfreezing Trauma* lends a dual perspective that would be a great tool for EMDR clinicians."
Shana Bombrys, EMDR Therapist

"In *Unfreezing Trauma*, we are invited into Mary J. Held's past. We are welcome guests, travelling with her into a once private journey of trauma, fear, learning, remembering, forgiving, and loving. Her courageous journey and strong desire to help others have given us a tool and a path to heal. Thank you."
Julie Dillon, Spirituality and Wellness Coach

UNFREEZING TRAUMA

UNFREEZING TRAUMA

MY PRIVATE JOURNAL OF EMDR RECOVERY

by
Mary J. Held

With Therapist Comments by
Nova Muir Green, M.S.W.

Fresh Streams Publishing Co. LLC Lansing MI
Edited by Robert Magnan and Janice LaRue

Unfreezing Trauma
Mary Judith Held

Copyright © 2019 by Mary Judith Held

All rights reserved. This book may not be reproduced in whole or part, stored in a retrieval system, or transmitted in any form or by any means electronic, mechanical or other without written consent from the writer, except by a reviewer, who may quote brief passages in a review.

First Edition 2020

ISBN: 978-1-7342691-0-9

IN MEMORIAM

Nova Muir Green

Words cannot express the love and sorrow.

DEDICATION

To those trauma survivors who have been willing to share their stories with me – Greg L, who told me of his recovery through EMDR, Annette A., Patty, Tonya, and Arron –and to all the people who spend their lives and their energy trying to escape from old visions. May you find your way out of the past!

ACKNOWLEDGMENTS

I would like to thank my friend and psychotherapist, the late Nova Muir Green, and my friend, Bob Magnan, who both helped me battle and gave me the support to persevere. I would also like to thank Rob Wipond, who planted the seed of the possibility of joy and watered it for years. The almost daily help I received from the 8:15 am twelve step meetings was invaluable. Thanks go to Carlton Hammond and Susan Dickey, who never gave up on the book, Janice LaRue who helped edit, and proofreader John Seymour. Finally, I thank all the therapists and friends who have tried to help victims of trauma.

CONTENTS

DEDICATION vii
ACKNOWLEDGMENTS vii
FOREWORD... xi
INTRODUCTION... 1
SESSION ONE 7
   NOVA'S COMMENTS ON SESSION ONE 10
      INTERVAL ONE 13
SESSION TWO... 21
   NOVA'S COMMENTS ON SESSION TWO 24
      INTERVAL TWO 27
SESSION THREE 41
   NOVA'S COMMENTS ON SESSION THREE.......... 43
      INTERVAL THREE.. 45
SESSION FOUR 55
   NOVA'S COMMENTS ON SESSION FOUR............ 56
      INTERVAL FOUR... 57
SESSION FIVE... 61
   NOVA'S COMMENTS ON SESSION FIVE 64
      INTERVAL FIVE 65
SESSION SIX 73
   NOVA'S COMMENTS ON SESSION SIX 74
      INTERVAL SIX 77
SESSION SEVEN.. 81
   NOVA'S COMMENTS ON SESSION SEVEN........... 83
      INTERVAL SEVEN.. 85
SESSION EIGHT 87
   NOVA'S COMMENTS ON SESSION EIGHT 88

INTERVAL EIGHT	89
SESSION NINE	99
NOVA'S COMMENTS ON SESSION NINE	102
INTERVAL NINE	103
SESSION TEN	109
NOVA'S COMMENTS ON SESSION TEN	111
INTERVAL TEN	113
SESSION ELEVEN	137
NOVA'S COMMENTS ON SESSION ELEVEN	138
INTERVAL ELEVEN	139
SESSION TWELVE	151
NOVA'S COMMENTS ON SESSION TWELVE	152
INTERVAL TWELVE	155
SESSION THIRTEEN	173
NOVA'S COMMENTS ON SESSION THIRTEEN	177
INTERVAL THIRTEEN	179
SESSION FOURTEEN	187
NOVA'S COMMENTS ON SESSION FOURTEEN	189
INTERVAL FOURTEEN	191
SESSION FIFTEEN	195
NOVA'S COMMENTS ON SESSION FIFTEEN	195
INTERVAL FIFTEEN	197
SESSION SIXTEEN	201
EMDR RESOURCES	207
OTHER RESOURCES	209

FOREWORD

How does it feel to live with trauma, to be afraid to leave the house, to have flashbacks, to be convulsed by seizures? And then how would it feel to recover from years of that in only four months?

In this book Mary Judith Held shares her experiences working through psychotherapy to recover from traumatic incidents. More specifically, we follow Mary through psychotherapy sessions in which her therapist used eye movement desensitization and reprocessing (EMDR).

EMDR is a method developed in the 1990s by Francine Shapiro. In very simple terms, the therapist asks the client to recall distressing experiences and then directs the client in bilateral sensory stimulation, most commonly side-to-side eye movements. The goal of this stimulation is to change the way in which traumatic memories are stored in the brain and reduce the effects of traumatic experiences. EMDR has been effective in treating post-traumatic stress disorder as well as other mental illnesses.

Mary recounts each of her 16 sessions, often describing traumatic events in detail. Then, her therapist comments on that session. Between each session and the next, Mary shares what she wrote in her journal—her reactions to what she and her therapist did in that session and more generally what she felt, what she thought, what she realized about her experiences and herself.

That's what Mary is sharing in this book —her accounts of the therapy sessions, comments by her therapist, and her journal entries. But why?

She's going public with her experiences in the hope that others who have been victimized by physical violence and sexual abuse may benefit from her experiences with EMDR therapy and be inspired to keep working to recover from their own traumatic incidents. These people will understand what Mary experienced:

> The idea that things freeze and can be re-experienced again and again must be understood if anyone is to understand what is happening to me, and what I now know happens to other people. It is not just that horrible things happen to you. ... But for me and for many others, emotionally, those horrible things do not stop; these events feel part of our current lives.

A few years ago, Mary shared with me her journal entries as she was going through EMDR therapy sessions. It hurt to read them, to feel how she suffered, but I felt so happy that finally, after many years of therapy and coping mechanisms, she had found something that was helping her progress up her path of recovery.

It's very difficult for victims of traumatic incidents to talk about their experiences and their feelings with people close to them or with therapists. Inspired by the women who have dared to come forth with their stories in the #MeToo movement and most notably Dr. Christine Blasey Ford, Mary is showing great courage in sharing her experiences with thousands of strangers. I'm very proud of her for writing and publishing this book.

Robert Magnan

INTRODUCTION

This is the story of some traumatic incidents that happened to me, how they affected my life, and how EMDR gave me my life back.

First, a little background. I was born in Ohio, the second of six children, the oldest girl in my family. We were very Catholic and I was smart. I went to eight years of Catholic grade school and got a full scholarship for four years of a Catholic high school. I then won a full four year scholarship to any college in the continental United States. I ended up at Michigan State University, and graduated after four years with a B.A. in anthropology and a minor in sociology/social work. I went into social work.

Drinking had been a problem since my first drink in high school, and it progressively got worse. After two years at the social work job, I dramatically quit over some perceived disagreement, but it was actually because I had chosen drinking over work. I drank daily and I was mostly unemployed for the next three years. In 1977, I had a child and got sober. I went back to MSU and earned a B.S. in math, and soon started teaching math. After I'd been teaching at various places for seven years, I signed up for a special program teaching in the United Arab Emirates. After three years there, in 1993, my son and I came back to the States, I started having seizures, and we ended up in Michigan.

By November, 2004, I was living by myself in Lansing, Michigan, able to work only nine hours a week at the local community college. I had been sober 27 years and attended 12-step meetings about three times a week. Those were the main activities in my life, that 14 hours or so. Every moment of those hours was scheduled, painstakingly timed, to take advantage of the brief times when my body was not thrashing about in the seizures that started ten years before.

Those ten years since the seizures started had been full of doctors and counselors. At first, it was diagnosed as stress and the treatment was yoga, swimming, walking, talk therapy and some drugs. When that didn't work, it was suggested that I move back to be near my family in Ohio, and I did. The doctor there sent me to the neurologists who diagnosed it as epilepsy, and the drugs became much stronger, with harsh side effects on the body. When a test taken while I was seizing disproved that diagnosis, it was back to psychiatrists and a new idea, conversion disorder. That seemed to me to be a non-diagnosis, since it was what the doctors and psychiatrists called it when they couldn't find any physical reason for symptoms. My latest psychiatrist simply added more drugs to my regimen and put me in talk therapy. By that time, I was so drugged up that I was always exhausted and still having seizures. He threatened to have me committed unless I took even more meds, so I agreed, then played "bad patient" and missed appointments until I got a new insurance and immediately changed to a new psychiatrist. This gentle man worked with me to get off all the drugs. Then, through almost obsessive tracking of behavior, we found a way we could predict when I would be seizure free. After five years of not working, I was able to work six, then nine hours a week at a local preschool. I moved back to Michigan and started teaching again at the community college where I'd worked before I went to the Middle East.

So at the start of November, 2004, that is where I was. My only child, Jon, had married a woman earlier in the year that I really liked, but she seemed to change as soon as they were married. Their problems and eventual divorce led to my son's attempted suicide in early November. Because of how I dealt with his suicide attempt, my ability to work diminished. Everything was getting harder and harder. I was losing the battle for my life.

Then towards the end of November, something happened. I was seizing at a 12-step meeting. A man, Greg, touched my arm lightly and the seizure calmed down. After the meeting, he talked to me about this therapy that he had undergone, called EMDR – Eye Movement Desensitization and Reprocessing. It had changed his life. Greg recommended a book on the subject, David Grand's

Emotional Healing at Warp Speed, and gave me the name of his therapist. He believed it would help me.

****

It took me until late January 2005 to build up the energy to read the book and what I read amazed me. The story that still sticks in my mind is of a train engineer who had hit and killed someone on the track. The person had jumped in front of the train to kill himself. The engineer knew he was not at fault. But he could not stop seeing the body, could not stop reliving the moment of impact, the sound, the smell. He became unable to work.

Then he tried EMDR. It did not sound like much to me. He watched the therapist's fingers move from side to side; he moved just his eyes. Somehow that stimulated both sides of his brain in a way that let him relive the incident and notice things he had not noticed before. He realized emotionally what he knew intellectually, that he was not at fault. In his words, "It's over. In the past. I can go on now."

I wanted that. I knew about endlessly reliving traumas. I had some incidents in my life that whenever I thought about them, by chance or when a new therapist wanted to talk about them, I would be back there. Everything would be the same; the pain never left. I wanted that to be over. I had no idea if this EMDR was related to the seizures or not, but Greg believed it was and I supposed it could be possible. Afraid of yet another disappointment, it took a while to work up my courage to try yet another thing, but finally I called the therapist Greg had recommended.

That therapist did not take my insurance and I could not afford him. He started me on a trail of recommendations. One after another, the recommended therapists told me they were sorry, they didn't accept my insurance. Each would suggest another person to call, but nobody could help.

I knew I had to do something, had to persist. I decided to give myself a treat and called Nova, an old friend of mine, to invite her to dinner. I could manage that kind of excursion only about once every two months, so I did not see her often.

I told her about my search for an EMDR therapist. I was explaining to her that I had an income tax refund coming that I could use for a few sessions, when I noticed the expression on her face. "I've had training in EMDR," she told me." I will be glad to do it with you."

We set up a time to begin and she dropped off some information in advance. I learned that EMDR therapy begins with picking an incident and examining your feelings about that incident. Deep inside, what do you truly believe? How deeply do you believe that? That's called the *negative cognition*. What would you like to truly believe? How much do you believe that now? That was the *positive cognition*. I learned about finding a safe place to go in my mind when it became too painful and scary to go on with the therapy. I knew of three incidents that just thinking about could send me into what I called the black hole. I knew how I felt and how I would rather feel. I was ready to go.

****

At the very first session, Nova asked me to keep a journal of the sessions and of my thoughts and feelings between sessions. Sometimes I wrote in my journal several times a day; sometimes I went a day or two without journaling. Whenever I felt something new, noticed something different, I wrote about it.

I shared the journals with Nova and two other people – Bob, my true love from freshman year in college, and Rob, a good friend from the years when I was teaching in the Middle East, in the United Arab Emirates. Bob had found me after 32 years about the same time as I started EMDR therapy, and I shared the journal entries with him daily in our email correspondence. I sent Rob the journal entries on a more irregular basis, enough to enable him to keep track of me. Sometimes I added my conversations with Bob and Rob to the journal.

The sessions with Nova were two to three hours long and we met usually once a week. All the sessions after the first started with my reading the week's entries to Nova.

What follows are excerpts of the entries from my journal, pretty much exactly as I wrote them, with an occasional note in brackets to explain details. There were many things I did not know about myself when I started, and these came out during the process, sometimes quickly and painfully, sometimes slowly, like clues to a mystery. The journal entries follow the same order as the sessions and report the things I learned as they were uncovered and as my idea of myself and my life twisted and turned and changed. Each of my descriptions of the sessions is followed by Nova's comments. She adds not only expertise and a different perspective, but also another memory— many of the things she noticed in the sessions I do not remember at all.

SESSION ONE

Saturday, February 26

Nova came over this morning, and we did the first EMDR session on the "incident" with Alex. What a thing to call things I think of and am afraid, terrified, in danger of being sucked into the black hole. We talked about which experiences we could pick from. Holding the thoughts of all of them together was crazy making. I had to finish the thought, the emotion, of an incident and close it before I went on to another. Nova and I picked my safe place to go if things got bad; I would envision myself leading the children in singing at the Children's Mass when I had been living and teaching in the United Arab Emirates (UAE) in the Middle East.

I think I picked the incident with Alex because my stomach kept hurting, and stomach pain was such a part of that incident. I told her all the details that I could remember, which I have been over in therapy and with myself many times.

I was an active alcoholic at the time and I was living with a female lover, Ora B, and her two girls. Alex was Ora B's brother and had been staying with us for a month or so. I had slept with Alex, but we weren't really together. Ora was my true love, not Alex.

That night, Alex seemed to have forgotten that. He came home drunk and expected me to have the money to pay the cab driver. He was furious when I didn't.

Start of Session

Negative Cognition: I am a target for evil, and I drew what happened to me. Belief: highest value on the scale

Positive Cognition: I am no more a target than anyone else. Belief: lowest value on the scale

We start the EMDR, the fingers waving back and forth, my eyes following them.

I'm sitting on the couch in the living room when Alex comes home. He has taken a cab and wants me to give him the money to pay for it. I don't have the money. I don't know how the cab driver got paid. I am sure Ora B and the girls weren't home, or none of the rest of it would have happened. So Alex is really mad at me, and yells and then hits me. Well, I wasn't going to take that! I hit him back. An accelerated fight, a way of showing how angry you are. That's what I thought.

That is not what Alex thought. He had an incredible body, very muscular and strong, although he was only 5' 8" or so. He wanted to do serious harm to me and he could.

I don't know how long we tussled before I ended up on the ground. I remember lying in the fetal position and him kicking me with those big platform shoes again and again. I wasn't fighting anymore. I was just trying to stay alive.

He screamed at me the whole time and called me names. It might have been his repeating "You dirty bitch" that made him think of the bath, think of cleaning me from my supposedly disgusting behavior.

The bathtub was upstairs. He dragged me up the stairs slowly as I was fighting. I knew I wasn't going to like whatever was coming. But he got me into the bathroom and kept screaming at me while he filled the tub with scalding hot water. I could see the steam rising from the tub and remember him telling me that it will burn my skin. I think I am going to die.

I don't know if I was fully clothed, but for some reason he let go of me while he was paying attention to the tub and I saw a chance.

I raced down the stairs, out the front door, and across the small one-lane street to the neighbors' house. I knew them to speak to, but we weren't friends. I burst into their house screaming and grabbed the large newel post at the beginning of the stairs.

I remember her looking at me. Her husband was there, but I don't remember much about him. It is only today that I can see their children, called by the commotion from their bedtime routine. They were in pajamas; the one closest to me as I clung to the pole had on footed pj's.

And Alex was there, telling them that I had taken some bad acid, that I was having a bad trip, that he would take me home. She bent down and tried to pry my fingers off the pole, tried to get me out of her house. I was frantic, I was hysterical, and she didn't believe that Alex was trying to kill me.

So I asked her to call my friend Phyllis, gave her the number, and said she would come and get me, but please not to let Alex take me because he would kill me.

It is only now that I know she wasn't to blame. They were getting ready for bed and here is a half-naked hysterical woman screaming and crying and attached to her stairs.

The police were not our friends in that neighborhood. From where I am now, the police are easy to call, are the people to call, but at that time, in that place, they weren't. But she did call Phyllis, who came and took me.

I don't know what all I told her or what all she believed about that night. She took me to my old college roommate Susan's house, where I think I slept on the floor. The next day I couldn't eat because my stomach hurt so much. I didn't have insurance so Phyllis lent me her Medicaid card and I went to the hospital and said I had been beaten up coming out of a bar the night before. Nothing was broken; I was just bruised up pretty bad. I would get better.

But it has been, I now realize, at least 28 years since that happened. For the first time, thinking and writing about lying on the floor frantically gripping the pole doesn't send me into the feelings I had then. It doesn't suck me into the black hole, the place of unending despair and total pain. The tears that are falling at this moment are for the younger me who was so hurt, who didn't really deserve it, and sadness at the years the experience has lived in and waited for me and that I knew would return [to haunt me].

I can feel the difference in my body about the Alex incident. Alex is over. He was an evil man and it was not my fault. I was just in the wrong place at the wrong time and caught his anger at the world. He went to jail later for raping someone.

The role of the neighbor woman is the most surprising outcome from this. For years she has been part of refusing to help me like the rest of the world. But she was just a housewife putting her kids to bed. I was the hysterical one. Alex was calm and cool as he told his story. It made sense for her to believe him, makes even more sense that she would want me out of her house. Still she had enough empathy to call Phyllis. And my friend was used to me being a drunk who got into trouble and needed to be rescued. We lived outside the world where our parents had raised us. We were in a world where no questions needed to be asked or answered when we said to each other that we needed help.

End of Session

Negative Cognition: I am a target for evil, and I drew what happened to me. Belief: lowest value on the scale

Positive Cognition: I am no more a target than anyone else. Belief: highest value on the scale

[It is a complete reversal of where I started.] Will this relief last? My eyes have been mostly dry as I write. I have been able to think [the attack] through and write it down without terror. That time was not my fault. I do not know that about the other terrors in my past. I do not know that the world is safe or that I am not a target for the evil ones who live there. But I wasn't to blame for what Alex did. It was a thing that should not happen to anyone and no one should have to live through many times, even after it is over.

NOVA'S COMMENTS ON SESSION ONE

What isn't included in the preceding description of the EMDR session is Mary's emotion expressed during the telling. She groaned when she said she was kicked. She wept and yelled when Alex was pulling her upstairs. She cried and begged the neighbor to believe her, to please telephone her friend. Throughout the sessions it was a little daunting for me to be the instrument that elicited these deep and fierce and frantic feelings.

After the EMDR part of the session was over, which happened after the neighbor agreed to call Phyllis, Mary described the immediate changes she felt. She seemed immensely relieved, wondering, and joyous. She was so happy that the neighbor woman was no longer another example of the hostile world. She enjoyed feeling empathic with the woman's dismay and confusion when she and Alex came into her pleasant domestic world. But one expression of relief Mary repeated several times. "It wasn't my fault!" She didn't have to carry the blame for the abuse she'd received. She didn't "draw evil" to herself.

INTERVAL ONE

Saturday, February 26

5:00 pm, 5 hours after the session

Right now, I can think about the whole thing with Alex and just be sad that it happened, and angry that I had to tell this again and again trying to get relief, and no relief came. I feel 20 pounds lighter than I did this morning when I woke up. Is it possible that the "Preacher" incident will become the same thing, that I will be able to write about it someday without the terror? Maybe that will be the next [incident we discuss].

Like touching a sore tooth, I touch the memories of terror-filled times. I think of another time, and it still scares me… but maybe not as much as it used to.

6:45 p.m

I think I needed some beauty after this morning. I am listening to the CD of the Mozart performance I was part of in my hometown, Hamilton, [Ohio]. It strikes me that being in the middle of the choir and part of this wondrous noise would be a safe place. I think about asking Nova if she would like to go to the Mozart festival in Hamilton this April. Maybe Cathy, a friend of mine in Chicago, [my 12- step sponsor] would like to go with us. I should get the score from this and sing along with it like I do with the *Messiah*. It is wonderful. I think of this as what I should do when I get well.

Fighting the thoughts of being well is a very loud male voice warning me that I'll never get there, that I can't, it's not possible. I'll never get there, and the voice will keep me from it.

Sunday, February 27

6:30 a.m.

When I check quickly lying in bed this morning, the Alex incident seems like something that happened long ago. I start to think about other traumatic incidents , but leave that thought quickly and think of how little I am in most of my thoughts about childhood.

In school I was always the littlest, and I hated that. I remember a girl in the fourth grade who came from somewhere else and left after that year but was my best friend – she was shorter than me. You always know this in Catholic school, because they tend to put you in lines according to size, to go to church in the morning, for processions, that kind of thing. It just occurs to me that I was shorter than everyone in grade school because I was the youngest in my class. That was why! I never connected those two things before. My mother had the choice of sending me to kindergarten, which was where my age would have placed me in the public schools, or first grade at St. Ann's. St. Ann's changed the age to conform with the public schools soon after that. Mom thought I was too smart for kindergarten.

At this moment it looks like the one thing falling into place from yesterday is a peripheral one of size. I'm no longer shorter and smaller than everyone else. I caught up [years later] when we all stopped growing taller.

5:00 p.m.

Just got back from the library. Feeling taller and lighter, but also fat, like maybe I'm living in my real body now. Feeling really sad for the little girl I was. She had a hard time, little thing. I felt very unsafe at the library, looking around like the anti-terrorist guys taught me in the UAE. Couldn't stay there long. Got a few things, started feeling shaky like I would go into a seizure. Still stayed long enough to check online to see when the community college is having spring break. Next week, not this week. So hopefully tomorrow morning I'll be good to go for work.

I hope so.

Monday, February 28

2:30 p.m.

Didn't really think I'd make it to work this morning, but I did okay. I'm still tired and subdued and not too interested in talking to anyone or seeing anyone. This morning I was still sad for the little girl and felt like crying, worried that I might start crying at work. But then I concentrated on the students I would help and asked for some help to stay in the moment, to be okay. I made it.

I'm still feeling lighter. It is now after my after-work nap and I don't really want to see anyone or talk to anyone. I'm reading a book, a holiday romance novelette actually, and the woman has had a miscarriage and can't move past it. It now makes me kind of angry that people don't know it's not intentional [that you don't lose that intense awareness], that [the incident] is locked in place somehow, and that talking about things sometimes just makes you relive them, without changing the feelings.

I don't know if I'm finished with the Alex thing yet, but I know I am tired of it.

Wednesday, March 2

5:45 a.m.

Still feeling taller. Thinking about how the three big traumatic incidents from that time may have happened in the same year, which may be why they froze. Too much to process too quickly. Susan, my roommate from college comes into the story with Alex, and I was thinking yesterday about a male friend from college. He wasn't around for the Alex thing, but he was for one of the other ones. It just seems like my memory in terms of time is becoming clearer.

The thing with Alex was about a person, not about the whole world. I feel sad and tears are getting close. I still think about how the couch looked from lying on the floor while he was kicking me. I will talk to Nova about that.

10:25 a.m.

Sometimes I really resist doing this, all this writing and thinking, and sometimes I get carried away. It seems to be getting harder as the days go by. The thing that strikes me is the whole "how I view my life" thing. My drinking time and experiences subjectively are a giant chunk, like 100 years in hell. In reality, I just noticed last month, when I reconnected with Bob, that the bad drinking time started when I quit my job as a social worker (1974) and ended when I got sober (1977). That's only three years, not 100. Time seems to be rearranging somewhere in my head. I've been wondering how long I was with Ora. It's always felt like years, but if the drinking was only really bad for three years, it could not have been even three years. That makes me nervous to think about, and I suspect that it is going to be a shock to me when I tie the three incidents down to the calendar.

When I check [in my mind] on the Alex incident now, it's not the idea that it is past, which it seemed to be earlier, but just sadness that it was something that shouldn't have happened.

I knew I needed to get this down before it morphed into something else, and I made a deal with myself – if I wrote it down, then I got to play Legend of the Green Dragon online for a while. So I'm off to play!

Thursday, March 3

7:00 a.m.

I just noticed last night how disorganized my house is, how messy. I looked at my checkbook and noticed that I hadn't balanced last month's statement, and then couldn't find it. Last month's book club card hadn't been sent in. I went through two Sunday papers this morning.

For the last two days, my focus has been off. I start something, and then forget about it. Preheat the oven and forget to put in the food. Load the coffee maker and forget to turn it on. Even this morning, I got out my socks and then got distracted before I put them on by clothes that hadn't made it to the hamper, and then lost the socks. I got out the milk to have a glass and wandered off, leaving the milk out and the glass empty. I wonder what this is about.

The almost-ready-to-cry thing is here now and has been [since I woke up]. My best guess is that I am just taking in the Alex thing. I know that it is over, that it is past, that it has a much different feel than the other incidents.

Friday, March 4

6:55 a.m.

I'm feeling connected this morning, which is good since I go to work in a little bit. Nova and I will be getting together tonight, and I'm ready for it. House is messier than usual, but hey! I managed to get the laundry done yesterday! Didn't forget to turn it on, or put in the soap, or anything.

Nova and I will talk about the journal tonight when she gets here. She's bringing her schedule so we can block out the next four or five sessions. I vacillate between wanting to do one of the "big" incidents and wanting to do something that is at least removed in time from the drinking terrors. The only thing that motivates the desire for a big thing is that I have next week off, so I can be totally weird for a whole week.

The time frame is still getting into place. As I think of the house I was in and how old my friend Phyllis's daughter Beth was at the time of these events, the time [in which the incidents occurred] gets shorter. I am thinking I was lucky to survive it all relatively intact.

I need to go to work.

10:40 a.m.

Didn't make it through three hours at work; I started a seizure and had to leave. Things are still rearranging themselves in my head. It is disconcerting to feel so much taller. I actually perceive people as being shorter than they have been. It is a subtle change, but it is important and amazing. I think about or remember things and they are different than they were last week, or yesterday, or a few minutes ago. The landscape of my life is altering. I did not understand this very well from the literature on this [EMDR] process.

People go through my mind, and my relationship to them has changed. The fan club has dissolved, that strange place where I put people who thought I was wonderful, dismissing them as a "fan club" of folks who were incredibly bright and interesting and had one flaw that I saw – they had an inflated idea of me. It felt like a revelation when I discovered inside me some time ago the existence of that club. Yes, I am a person who has a much different way of experiencing and examining the world than many others, and I have been blessed in my life by finding other people who are as incredible in their own way as I am. Wow, that was a backhand "I am an incredible person," and I know it and I believe it and it is true.

No wonder I had a seizure and had to leave work! I had more pressing things to think about, to get down before they floated away or morphed while I wasn't watching them.

I had been starting to think of myself as alone, friendless, and not wanting friends, which seemed pretty odd but true last week. It is not true. I have some incredible friends, some of whom are sharing this experience with me and some not.

I've also been thinking about the subconscious. Many years ago my friend Rob brought up the idea that the subconscious was a place where we chose to store things, not a place like an arm or a leg that is just part and parcel of us, but a place that we create by refusing to look at things. If it weren't for repression of ideas, thoughts, and emotions, the subconscious would not exist.

I don't know if I believe that. I do see why there is some concern in the literature about what the EMDR process does to people. What does it mean when a series of eye movements releases pivotal experiences frozen in the brain and reintegrates them [into time with the rest of my memories]? Where does the depth of life come from unless from these intensely experienced events?

I know it is people who have *not* had these things take over their lives who worry about this [loss of intensity]. I want to find everyone I know who has had a trauma affecting them in their day-to-day life and tell them to do EMDR right away!

When I think back quickly on my life, I remember things that were pivotal and joyous. Rolling down a hill behind the Kellogg Center, the on-campus hotel and conference center. That was my first year in college. We were all small-town kids with incredible intelligence who had just discovered they were not alone in the world. The giggly wonder of new love that was Bob.

The incident with Alex was sad and something we should work hard as a civilization to prevent. But it is getting integrated into my life as a memory [from long ago] rather than a current event. The fact that EMDR can unfreeze it doesn't mean that it means nothing, [that it is okay on any level that it happened].

I'm tired, and hungry, and want a cigarette. But I'm okay.

SESSION TWO

Saturday, March 5

We started with my reading the journal out loud to Nova, and we talked about it some. She agreed it was all pretty amazing. We talked about the couch that I had mentioned in the journal, and as we talked it wasn't really about Alex at all. It was about the rest of the house, the coffee table, the big statue of a panther that Ora had – the rest of my life there. I had been happy in that house as well.

After reading the journal, we chose to work with the time I tried to tell my mother something I thought she would not want to hear. Her brother, my 21-year-old uncle, had taught me about oral sex. I knew it was our secret, but it wasn't until I read the little examination of conscience book we used before confession that I knew God had an opinion about it. So I told the priest about seeing the secret and sacred parts of someone else's body. The priest had asked for particulars and I gave them to him. He told me I had to go right home and tell my mother about it. He was very upset and very stern when he made me promise to do this right away.

Start of Session

Negative Cognition: I am helpless and no one would help me, no one protected me. Level of belief: medium value on the scale

Positive Cognition: I can ask people for help. Level of belief: didn't believe it at all, lowest value on the scale

Nova starts moving her fingers back and forth and I start to remember.

I'm five, maybe six years old. I'm standing in the kitchen looking up at Mom. I'm near the doorway, about eight feet from her. She is in front of the stove. George, around one, is sitting on her hip; she has one arm around him. She's wearing a dress, and hanging onto her skirt wanting something is one of the other little ones, either Chuck or Betty. I think she's cooking fried chicken. I know that's the chicken pan on the stove, and she has a fork in her hand turning something. Some kind of meat, for sure. The potato pan is bubbling away.

I stand there for a while looking at her. My poor mama. She has so much to do and all these little kids always around her wanting things. Hanging on her all the time. There are six of us -- John, eight years old, next is me, Anna would have been four and then the little ones, Chuck (three), Betty (two), and George (one). She works so hard, all the time, and it is my job to help her.

I know that telling her this won't help her. I know the priest told me she has to know. But it will cause trouble, and I don't want to cause my mama more trouble. I don't want to be like those little kids who are trouble all the time. She will be mad at her brother, she will be mad at me, she will have a very bad time. I don't want to do this to my mother.

I am now an adult standing behind my little girl and I am amazed at how young my mother is. She's about eight years older than Jerry, so around 29. Her face is unlined, her hair soft and brown, her eyes clear. She is my mama, but a young mama, working harder than she should have to. I feel for her and I feel for me and what I see as my job. I will handle this myself.

I didn't do anything right away. I went to confession again and the priest asked me if I had told my mother. I didn't know they were allowed to remember you from other times. I had decided not to do what the priest told me to, and this was a hard thing for a little Catholic girl to do. But I wasn't going to hurt my mom. I avoided him, and was very glad when he got moved to another parish.

The next thing I remember vividly is how I actually did get him [my uncle] to stop. I don't know exactly when. I am still not very tall. I am dusting the bedroom floor, and the dust mop handle looms above me. I just finished dusting under the big double bed when my uncle comes in. I know what he wants.

I'm feeling very virtuous. I'm doing a good job and even got under the bed, and now he wants to do bad things. So I tell him, very firmly, very clearly, that God does not like this, and we can't do it anymore. It seems to me that I look straight ahead when I say this, and my dust mop is like a giant defensive weapon at my side. I have no doubt that this is the right thing to do.

He never touched me again after that.

What a little soldier I was! I have a vision of me with a little pointy helmet on my head, like the kids in *The Lion, the Witch, and the Wardrobe*.

Tied in to how I feel about this is the book *In Garments All Red* about St. Maria Goretti. This let me know exactly how wrong it had been, she made a man stab her 16 times rather than give in, and forgave him before she died. This was all an incredibly important thing to avoid. I don't know if that was before I told my uncle it had to stop or not. I can't imagine the school giving us that book, telling us that story, in second grade.

Is it possible that most of the bad feelings came from other people's judgments? Nova said that I decided I should take care of the problem, and I took care of the problem. I did save my mother from going through all that and got myself out of the situation. My uncle moved back in with his father not long afterwards, and I don't remember being afraid that he would go after my sisters. I would have been watchful if I suspected.

Through the years I have been in counseling of various kinds and it is a standard question to ask about sexual abuse. I have had many counselors tell me my mother should have been there, that I was too young and should have told her. Maybe they are wrong. Maybe I was right. The various activities with my uncle never scared me or hurt me and were usually just kind of weird. That wasn't a big trauma.

I was a little mother in that house. I helped with the kids, set the table, mashed potatoes, made the coleslaw, cleaned. I was a competent little person at home. Then I went to school and I was just a little insignificant thing. I wouldn't talk to them [teachers or students]. The [teacher] told my mother that I whispered instead of talking loudly. At school, they put me in the hall and made me talk loudly so they could hear me. It wasn't about being loud; it was about being nothing at school when I was an important part of the family at home. I didn't like those other children.

I never ceased being a power at home throughout grade school. I remember my sister Anna, a year and a half younger than me, two grades behind me in school. She had volleyball practice a long way from home, at a school close to a mile away. It was dark when practice was over. I would walk there to meet her, to keep her safe on the way home. I didn't think about being in danger. I totally believed in myself and I had to take care of her.

Nova and I had to change the positive cognition. It wasn't, for me at the time, that I couldn't get help from my mother. It was me wanting to protect her, and all the other stuff about what should and shouldn't be true and right, what I should have done or should have been able to do, that is other people's stuff. Mostly I wanted to help my mom, and that is what I did.

End of Session

Negative Cognition: I am helpless. Level of belief: do not believe at all

Positive Cognition: I was a strong little girl who could help herself and her mother. Level of belief: totally believe it, highest on scale.

NOVA'S COMMENTS ON SESSION TWO

When Mary told me she had to find someone who could do EMDR with her, the problem she found unendurable was fear. She was afraid to go to the store, afraid to drive her car at night, afraid to go to work. She said, "I'm almost afraid to leave my house, to go out in my yard!" She said every move needed hours of encouragement before she could force herself to act. Mary also had flashbacks to some terrifying episodes that happened to her in her early 20s. She believed that these episodes had a great deal to do with her present enslavement to fear. That is the reason we began the sessions with her encounter with Alex.

However, in the second session, she suddenly started talking about her childhood and "how short I was." She remembered the experience with her uncle and how she handled it. Mary said she had told the story to a number of therapists and it was interpreted as an occasion when she was deprived of the loving concern she needed. I said that wasn't the way she told the story during EMDR. She described an independent little girl, the oldest girl, the second mother, looking at her mother, thinking, "My poor mama. She has so much to do and all these little kids always around her wanting things. Hanging on her all the time. ... She works so hard, all the time, and it is my job to help her. I know that telling her this won't help her."

Mary could have had all kinds of concern from her mother, but that brave and independent little girl didn't want to give her mother one more thing to worry about. She wasn't "one of those little kids who just are trouble all the time." The little Mary decided to take care of the situation by herself and did!! Mary in the present said, "YES! That's really the way it was. That's how I felt." There is extra information in EMDR therapy, not just word pictures, but a drama acted out before the therapist that can make interpretation a description rather than an educated guess.

The emergence of the "brave little girl" was very important to Mary and led to a number of stories later about her fearlessness. Mary asked her sister for a picture of her at that age, and has it in a frame beside her computer, watching and approving as Mary writes about her feelings in the intervals between sessions.

INTERVAL TWO

Saturday, March 5

11:30 a.m.

I just got back from the library, and I took the strong little girl with me. I could envision her walking by my side, with her little helmet on, ready for battle. I know that little girl was me and wonder where I lost her. She was strong and brave and determined.

I am thinking about life as a child. I can see more, and it is more fun. We were so very stable. We had the same pots and pans, seems like my entire life. When I first went out on my own and had to cook for myself, it was hard to gauge amounts, because I was used to using the pots as the measure. Fill it with whatever until it is so deep in the pot.

Nova asked me to look for pictures of myself as a first grader. I think most of them are with my Dad, but I looked in one of my two trunks here. Found my fourth-grade class picture. There she is, the girl who was shorter than me. What a little cutie she was! There were 50 kids in my class. I didn't remember there being so many. And I don't look that far out of the range, just at the little end of it. Some of those girls were giant! I remember that one of my best friends was about twice my size. My mom always laughed when she saw us together.

I keep thinking of times I was strong as a little girl. That was another thing that was so different in first grade! Girls could be mean and nasty to each other and not be called to account for it. In the neighborhood, if you made one of the little ones cry, you got beat up. Period, end of story. That was the neighborhood code. But the Catholic kids lived mostly closer to the school than we did. Our neighborhood was a little iffier and was mostly Protestant kids. There were several Catholic families, but none who had girls in my grade. So those girls in school could be rude and exclusive and mean to me, and not only was there no one to protect me, I couldn't just go knock them down for it.

Such power that was in the neighborhood!! Nobody ever got hurt so bad that they went to the hospital but we fought. I remember a boy who lived for a while down by the railroad tracks, a few blocks from my house. Anna was friends with his sister, and he made Anna cry. I had to go beat him up for that; since he was a grade behind me, he was much too young for John. Years later, when I was an amazingly arrogant, very well-developed teenager, he tried to walk home with me. After I had beaten him soundly at an early age! No chance for him.

The whole neighborhood was that way, our little four-square-block piece of the world. Once, this little girl bit Anna so hard she drew blood. She was actually Anna's age, so I shouldn't have gotten involved. But she had drawn blood! So I went after that girl, holding her face down on the ground and pummeling her little back.

She had a big brother, who took exception to this. He was a giant among children, or so it seemed to me. He was way older than John, even, so he must've been eight years older than me. He came down to my house to get me. The big guns came out, Mom chased him down the street, hitting him around his shoulders, I think with a broom, yelling at him. I can see it now. Go, Mom!

Yeah, stories of power. I got cornered once by a boy I didn't really know. We were playing some kind of game where you took prisoners, and there were two teams. He was on the other side and captured me in the stairwell leading to a basement room in the public school down the block from us. It was enclosed; the building came out over the stairwell. I remember standing down there, looking up at him. I didn't like the way he looked at me, and for a moment, I was afraid. Then I started planning. The concrete enclosing the stairwell ended, and there was some kind of fencing material on top of it. Then there was a gap, not very big, but hey, I wasn't very big. So I started just going up and down the stairs, letting him get used to my motion, until I lulled him into not paying attention. Then quick, up the little fence and through the little opening before the building started. I was free and left him in my dust.

What a strong, brave, smart little girl I was!

The neighborhood kids were the kids I understood, the kids who understood me. I always thought that the big division between my school person (called "Mary Judith" at first, later just "Mary" at St. Ann's) and the summer person called Judy, was that no one in the neighborhood knew that I was smart. As I think of it now, there are other things. No one at school lived by the same rules of fighting and protecting your family and friends that we did. They were not as independent as the kids in our neighborhood were expected to be, not as secure.

I keep thinking I'm going to run out of power stories. Here's one from later, when I was babysitting age, the summer I was 12 or 13. I was watching a family of seven kids. Their dad worked for the railroad and had a drinking problem; their mom, Betty T, was one of my mom's friends and kind of exotic to us. She was a flashy dresser and used makeup, and I think probably ran around with other men. She'd come over and hang out with my mom, the only woman I recall who ever did that. Anyway, I was watching the kids. Connie was towards the bottom, probably the fourth or fifth kid, a scrawny little girl whom her mom had expected to be a really girly-girl. She got that in her second-to-last child, Amy. Anyway, Connie was riding her tricycle around the block and a big boy knocked her down and started hitting her. Connie was maybe half his size, so she got a rock and hit that boy to make him stop. The boy's dad hit her and chased her home.

I don't know where I was when that was happening, maybe I had gone to the store, but when I got back with the littler kids she was hysterical, had crawled up on the fireplace mantel to hide. I got the story out of her and then we were off — me, all 5' of me, trailed by probably three or four little kids, off to see this grown-up who had hurt Connie for defending herself. I didn't know him, knew the kid only by sight, but up to the door we went, our little procession, knocked, and when he came to the door I gave him a serious talking to. He should have been ashamed of his son for hitting a little girl! Not hit her himself!

What happened to that fearless warrior?

Sunday, March 6

5:20 a.m.

Last night a woman came over that I have been working with in the 12-step program. She has been "out there" as we say, sober for a while, back into drugs, back into a rehab program, two days ago was using, wanted to yesterday and came to see me instead. This is a woman that I thought of as I read the EMDR literature – if this stuff does what it says, she needs it. I really am a little Catholic girl who had some rough times in life and got stuck there. (I can hardly believe I'm saying that! It's true. I know I have other things, [other incidents] but it is really true.) The point last night was that she has told me some stories that are more horrific than mine, lasted longer, lasted years. She needs this [EMDR].

She's sitting at my table, and we're talking about how you have to divide your time up, how you have to school your mind to think of only that period of time you can imagine not using. The big motto, of course, is "One Day at a Time." The reality in the beginning and at some intense times is one minute, five minutes, whatever you think you can live through without "taking the edge off." This woman knows the black hole.

And some "memories" are out to get her. And I use those quotes because there is a difference between these things and memories!

But let me tell what happened last night.

I wanted to give her hope. I wanted to tell her that it was true in a way that I didn't know before now that tomorrow can be profoundly different from today.

I told her an abbreviated version of the Alex story, rushing through "There was this guy who beat me up, knocked me down, kicked me, dragged me upstairs, got a burning hot bath ready for me …".

She interrupted. "Did he boil the water?"

She knew what this stuff was about. Some of them boil the water.

And she knew when, even in the fast version, the horror came. The escape, the hanging on to the pole, the neighbor woman trying to pry my hands off. The illusion of escape, the idea of freedom, and then [the terror] was back.

I told her what is only really impacting me this morning, that it was just a memory now. That something can happen that can take that away.

She's been through a lot more therapy than I have. Seemingly years of it, on a regular basis. For a while, they tried "desensitization," I think she called it, where they just kept taking her through the traumas again and again and again. It sounded like hell to me. She's been locked up a lot, in prison mostly. I talked to her about what was true for me now, that the incident is an incident, a memory, that it doesn't take me back there, that I don't relive it every time I tell it. That if I didn't know for sure that it terrorized me one week before, I wouldn't believe it.

I woke up this morning realizing how incredible it is, thinking that what I told her was true. I was off into trying to give her hope and not paying attention to what I was saying and feeling, not by myself and just looking at it.

That is what I am doing now. It is gone; it is part of a memory. This is what it must feel like in science-fiction books when the computer is implanted and you simply access all this stuff you didn't know. But I know that no one has been in my brain, that there was no drugs, no knife, no insertion of anything into my brain.

There was Nova's fingers, waving back and forth in measured pace. Me watching them. The two of us talking about whatever incident we picked, about Alex, about my mom, and then all she does is ask a question now and again, and move the fingers some more if I stop talking, and I'm there at the place we mentioned, and I see it all with new eyes.

The real point of the Alex story is that I got away, at the end, with my life and not even a broken bone. I got away, just like I got away from the guy who cornered me in that schoolyard stairwell. I got away and lived to tell the tale.

But all I have been telling myself, for over 28 years, all I have really felt and accessed is that horror in the pit of my stomach, that absolute terror, the one moment in *Psycho* where you say, "Oh my God! He is his mother!" — that very instant, again, and again, and again. People go there for fun, for amusement. It has been many, many years since I subjected myself to horror movies, because I know what they don't, that sometimes you get stuck there.

Seconds away from my neighbor changing her mind and making the call I was stuck. Mere seconds.

It changes my life in ways I will continue to notice. I think of the things yet to discuss, I think of the other terrors, and I know I can live through them, one more time, and they will finally be over.

10:30 a.m.

excerpt from email to Rob

I have to talk to you about this stuff. It is just incredible. I was just at a meeting, and the ideas were popping in my head so fast that I went into a seizure, like a computer that gets confused.

It is like you are an anchor to myself at some point in time. Bob, the other one the journals are going to, is an anchor in another time, but also pretty strong. Nova has known me for over 20 years and I feel safe with her. With all the rearranging happening in my head, I need to feel these anchors are strong.

I don't know if you are getting a real feel for this from the journal stuff. I can see why therapists are leery of it, it is much too fast. I can see the danger of it as well. It's like I've been laying somewhere and from where I am all I can see is this one ugly tree. The tree gets cut down, and all of a sudden, I see all of this other stuff, good stuff, beautiful trees and flowers and I don't know where I am and how I got there. I know that you and Bob and Nova are watching me and see that I haven't blown away to another land, that my life is still my life, but my reaction to it has changed.

Radically, incredibly, quickly.

I'm taller, I'm more aware of things, my interactions with people show me subtle changes in my attitude, in my memory, in my idea of myself. This procedure is so very simple, but the things it does!

Tuesday, March 8

9:30 a.m.

Just when I start thinking I'll have to wait for the next session to start things rolling, something shows up outside of the EMDR sessions.

I was at the [12-step] meeting this morning and someone was talking about all the things that don't happen to them since they've stopped drinking. Experiences started flashing through my mind, with the knowledge that those things were over. When it was my turn to talk, I talked about generic things. I haven't been beaten up. I haven't been raped. I haven't had to move and hide. I've been able to have a listed number. After I passed, [after it moved to someone else's turn to talk], I realized another thing that was over, the whole thing with a guy called Preacher.

As my drinking got worse, my choice of bars got worse. I could not stand to be at the bars where people had umbrellas in their drinks, where they left unfinished drinks on the table. I didn't want to be at places where people thought they were there to talk. We were there to get drunk; everything else was secondary.

One of the places I felt at home was at the sleazy bar next to the bus station. Serious drinkers started early in the morning, and we were serious about what we were doing. At the time, I thought I was better than them, for even in that crowd I wasn't the one buying early in the morning, I never bought before noon. I always got someone to buy me a drink.

I met a guy called Preacher. He was a giant of a man, kind of scattered, but good for drinks at 8 a.m. I vaguely remember him walking me home one time, or maybe he picked me up as I walked home. Anyway, he ended up knowing where I lived, and I ended up sleeping with him. Par for the course.

I knew that he was off, that sometimes he didn't seem to know who I was. He talked like we had been having a relationship for a long time, which wasn't true. He wanted me to have a phone and volunteered to get me one. I was living by myself. I left Ora B after I stole money from the kids' piggy banks to get drunk. I couldn't stand doing that kind of thing, taking advantage of little ones, so I decided to move. Neither Ora B nor the kids were as upset as I was about the money; they had wanted me to stay. I hadn't been there [in my new place] for very long. I was still deep into the "I'll sleep with anybody to get over my latest lost love" thing.

One night, Preacher came over and even for him he was strange. Usually he floated in and out of thinking I was someone else. This night he never really knew who I was.

And he was very pissed at this someone else. At first we didn't really acknowledge what was going on. The apartment was on the second floor and the stairway was in a little hallway by itself. From there you could get to all the other rooms in the house. So I started making up reasons to go from the living room to somewhere else, thinking about making a break for it. He just as nonchalantly blocked me.

We kept this up for a long time. He kept talking about things I hadn't done (things I knew nothing about) [and] berating me for them. Once in a while I tried to get him to see who I was, to realize that I wasn't the one he was talking to, but I was getting nowhere. He got more and more upset with me as the night went on.

Finally, in one of my wanderings, I got close enough to the stairs to try to break for it. He was incredibly tall and he was fast, faster than I thought, and he caught me.

It was now out in the open. He could talk openly about how I was not going to get away and started [talking] about what he was going to do with me.

I know there were things that he threatened before he got to his main theme, but I don't remember what they were. His main theme was we were going out to the country and he was going to cut off my head. He was going to grab my long hair and let my head swing in the air, free from my body. I believed he could do it.

He followed me everywhere in that little apartment. He kept it up; he was very attached to the thought.

And it went on and on and on. Sometimes it seemed he was slow to follow me and I would make a step towards the stairs. I once saw a cat playing with a mouse in a bathtub. She would let the mouse get away, but the mouse couldn't get up the sides of the tub, though he would frantically try. Then the cat would grab him again. This was the same scenario.

All night long he repeated the list of things that I would never do to him again, [things] I myself had never done, and then the head hanging from my body scenario. I got to the point where I almost wished we would leave and it would just be over because I couldn't stand one more moment of it.

Then the sun came up, and with the sun he changed. He would let me go this time; he would not take me to the country. He would just take me to the bedroom and fuck me for a while.

Eventually he was finished and left.

I took a bath and went to work. I couldn't stay there any longer. I liked my job. I ran a phone room, selling recreational property. When I had interviewed for the job, the two men who had interviewed me were drunk and were drinking during the interview itself. It had been great fun, and I had thought of going back there to continue drinking with them later that same day. But I just waited till they hired me. We used to drink all the time there -- beer in the morning, hard stuff at night after 9:00 p.m. when the girls working the phones had gone home.

I told my boss that I needed to leave town, that I had to leave right away. They were opening an office in Ann Arbor, [about 60 miles away], which is where my boss lived. He could move me there. We were, of course, having an affair, just part of being drinking buddies. So he got me an apartment there and two days later I moved. I stayed in a motel instead of my old apartment until I moved in at the new place.

It must have been Ora B who told me about Preacher. He was known to be crazy. He had once raped a woman in the middle of the street in broad daylight, and no one had done anything. He was strong and crafty and he took revenge. You didn't mess with him. Ora couldn't understand how I didn't know that.

Now I would have known that. Now, sober, I would have realized that a man who kept confusing me with some other white girl was not all there and potentially dangerous. What I wanted to say and didn't at the meeting this morning was that since I've been sober no one has threatened to cut my head off and let my head swing free from my body. I don't think I will ever have to put myself there again.

My strong little girl with her little helmet on her head is cheering for me.

11:00 a.m.

And so I went online to the Legend of the Green Dragon, I went to the land where the warrior girl lives, and affirmed that I am strong, not defenseless. While I may have been played with by the dragon who looked like a man, I was not defeated by him. I took up my weapons.

The victory is mine, the strength is mine. I do not need to look for protection or hide. I have the ability to see, judge, and avoid situations. If the time ever comes again when I am captured by the evil, I will survive. I did survive. I am healed but I am very sad. It was a very sad thing, a very bad thing, that should not happen. But this day I am free of him and the vision fades and takes its place in the past. It is over. It is done. The path there is growing over and is full of weeds. I will cease to water it and I will cease to travel it, for in traveling it I kept the path clear.

I am free. I just need to cry a while and let the weeds and sprouting trees of time grow.

Wednesday, March 9

6:00 a.m.

After I wrote all that yesterday, I started getting overwhelmed. My heart was beating really loud and fast. I was cold and felt like my head was going to burst, that I had to do something. Thoughts of another incident started coming back and I didn't want to go there. I tried walking around to release some of that energy, but it didn't work. I finally took a pill and calmed down.

I haven't talked to many people around me about this, but I did yesterday. My niece Beth called to see how I was doing, and I ended up telling her about some of it. She wanted to know if she knew any of the people involved. She knows at least one of them, her mom's old boyfriend, from a remaining incident, and she has stayed in touch with him. I don't want to change how other people feel about the people [involved], especially my uncle, and I also don't want Beth to know about her mom's old boyfriend.

Phyllis came over and I told her a little about what has been going on. I have been pretty reclusive since this [EMDR] started. I talked about the incident with Alex when she rescued me. "I remember," she said. "You thought he was going to put you in boiling water."

I didn't argue about whether it was real or not.

She told me that she thought I was with Ora B for around nine months. We lived elsewhere for a while, so the time for the incidents shortens. I feel uneasy. How could my idea of time be so wrong? I am scared, as though I am being stuffed into a box that is too small.

I need to do the Preacher incident with Nova. The vision is not defused; it still draws me and I don't want to go there. The thing with Alex doesn't feel the same. It is in the past and over. Preacher is going there but isn't there yet. It does not seem to work to go over these things without the EMDR.

Thursday, March 10

11:30 a.m.

Tonight is another session, and I am afraid of what might happen. I think about the fact that I have to be at work on Monday and I don't want to do that. Even with my brave little girl beside me I don't want to do anything, I want to just be ready to go with my mind, whether we are spinning quickly, racing to avoid something, going at warp speed through something, or just tired and sleepy.

Unfreezing Trauma

I was very tired yesterday. I took a nap, and still was in bed at 8:30 last night.

The Preacher thing will be the focus tonight. I know that, but I don't know what will happen.

I find a memory of moving to Ann Arbor after the incident. Susan, my old college roommate, her husband, and a friend who lived with them were all going to help me. Another friend had already shown up. It was a Sunday morning; I called Susan and she said that they'd be over as soon as they'd gotten their Sunday New York Times.

They never showed up. I don't remember anything about moving stuff from the old apartment. I don't remember even being in that place again, though I know I had things that went to Ann Arbor with me, so I must have been. I remember the lone friend who was helping me. Scenes shift in my head from moving into Ann Arbor and moving out of the old one. There is no sequence, just snippets.

The new place was a nice apartment complex, upscale, with a bar on the first floor. I could charge drinks to my room even. When I got to Ann Arbor, I found out fairly soon that I was pregnant. Preacher could have been the father. So could a number of other people, for I blanked Preacher out by replacing him with others.

I didn't believe it when the doctor told me I was pregnant. I had wanted to get pregnant by my ex, Tommy Walker, Beth's uncle. Tests had shown that the IUD I'd gotten from Family Planning had left me with scarred tubes. My chances of conceiving were slim to none. But I let them take a pregnancy test, convinced they would find just an inflammatory disease.

A nurse told me on the phone, and since I was single she asked if I wanted to talk about options to the pregnancy. I said no; I was thrilled that I was going to have a baby. I started reading to him, *Alice in Wonderland*, I think it was. But I didn't want to have the baby by myself in Ann Arbor. I wanted to go home to Lansing.

So I talked to my boss and moved back to Lansing. To a place not far from where Susan lived. I have quite an active imagination. There were alleys most of the way from Susan's house to my house, and I would walk back and forth between the two houses using those alleys. I would pretend that it was all a big forest. Only a few of the many houses that were actually there existed in my mind in the forest. There were things growing, and I pretended that I was strong, hiking in the forest. There was an overgrown rose bush in the alley that was gorgeous and lots of other flowers and bushes and trees. The actual alleys themselves were really like that, so they helped my imagining a lot.

    I am imagining my strong little girl telling me that I don't have to go on anymore right now. The story will wait; it is too hard right now. I will go on getting ready to slay the dragon again and then I will sleep.

SESSION THREE

Thursday, March 10

I read the journal [entries] to Nova, and we talked about some of it. She has always thought of me as the strong little girl, so the stories about power sounded right to her. The fear and hesitancy was what didn't sound right.

When I read about the Preacher incident, I was crying and could hardly see the page. I know I did that at the start of the session; those feelings were real. Now, as I write this after the session, they are not true.

Start of Session

Negative Cognition: They can find me. I am a mouse, and the cats recognize me. Belief: highest value on the scale

Positive Cognition: I am no more unsafe than anyone else. Belief: lowest value on the scale

She started moving her fingers, back and forth, adjusting the distance, and asking questions. I started talking; I have to watch her fingers carefully and look for the scene to unfurl.

Preacher is in the living room. He isn't really angry but lists all the bad things I supposedly did to him. I don't remember doing them. Possibly I did them in a blackout. Then he moves on to things I know I didn't do, but he doesn't believe me. I start to get scared, and I try to lull him into not paying attention, like I did with that boy in the stairwell long ago. It doesn't work.

He finally got angry about something. I can see him being angry at me, for something someone did to him, and that was when I tried to distract him and make it down the stairs. He grabbed me and took me into the living room. That was where we spent the night. He didn't let me out of there without being with me, not even to use the bathroom.

He rambled on about specific things I had supposedly done, when we were at a party and I treated him badly in front of his friends, that kind of thing. I think he was going through all the bad things any woman had done to him in his life. He said he should have beaten me then, he should have slapped me when I said whatever. I knew he wasn't talking about me, but I started apologizing. I said I was sorry, that he didn't deserve that. And he went on. Then he got to this favorite scenario. The ultimate punishment for all my misdeeds. He would kill me. He would cut my head off.

I don't know if he actually grabbed my hair and held it up and used his hand to show where he would slice it. I don't know if that is memory or my imagination kicking in as he described it. But he played with that idea a lot; he liked that idea. We would go in his car, he would find a place, slashing my head off was what I deserved for what I had done to him.

I can see the sun shining through the window, and he changed. He decided he wouldn't kill me. He would punish me another way and ordered me into the bedroom.

The biggest surprise during EMDR was remembering the feeling that raced through me when I walked into my bedroom with him behind me. HOORAY! All that is going to happen is I'm going to get raped. He's not taking me to the woods somewhere. I've won! I never before remembered the incredible triumph I felt when I realized I had won.

That flash was over in a second. This was my punishment, so I couldn't be glad! But I was glad! And didn't know it till now.

Nova and I just laughed. My joy at only being raped didn't come back until tonight, but I'm sure it came through somehow when I told others. How could they be sympathetic to the rape? I was describing the victory at the end as if it were the problem. The horror was the hours of listening to this very sick, very suspicious man go on and on about killing me in such a dreadful way. But I was very careful. I knew what could happen and that I could end up in those woods with him. And I made it!

End of Session

Negative Cognition: They can find me. I am a mouse, and the cats recognize me. Belief: lowest value on the scale

Positive Cognition: I am no more unsafe than anyone else. Belief: highest value on the scale

Nova was surprised at how it [cognition] changed so totally from "I feel like a mouse with a cat playing with me" to "He is a mouse who wants to be a cat, but he didn't get me." I think part of it is that she is such a believer in me and she trusts me to know what I am thinking and feeling. I cannot imagine many people who would laugh with me about the joy over being raped. What an idea! As she said, that was really letting someone else define my experience for me.

NOVA'S COMMENTS ON SESSION THREE

It was interesting to me that Mary described the whole incident with Preacher in the interval before the third session without getting any lasting relief from the memory. She had to repeat it during EMDR to free the trauma. The incident she described when she was young and trapped by a big boy on a stairwell came to me during the EMDR description of her night with Preacher. The young Mary said, "I didn't like the way he looked at me and for a moment I was afraid. And then I started planning." During that ghastly evening in her apartment, the older Mary remembered and tried the old technique, trying to lull his suspicions and then run to get down the stairs. But this time it didn't work. So she thought up another plan. She apologizes. She didn't argue that she had never done these things. She just told him again and again how bad she had been and how sorry she was and how she understood how he felt, on and on for all those hours. And finally, the sun rose, and his temper changed. He would be satisfied "this time!" with punishing her with rape. She had won!! She wasn't going to be killed! It was fascinating to hear her say, "I never before remembered the incredible triumph I felt when I realized I had won." Instead of him being the cat that played with and then killed the mouse, "he was a mouse who wanted to be a cat, but he didn't get me." I said to Mary, "and then you had the nerve to try to get sympathy for the rape!" We couldn't stop laughing. It seemed hilarious.

INTERVAL THREE

Friday, March 11

10:00 a.m.

Got up at 3:30 am this morning, and just kept thinking – couldn't sleep. Instead of writing I played online and had fun. At my morning [12-step] meeting we were talking about the promises of sobriety. "Fear of people will leave." That's the one I talked about. If I don't drink I don't go into locked rooms with crazy people.

We [Nova and I] started talking about the relationship between the seizures and the safety issue. I do not feel like a target anymore and that is incredible. My theory: I had some really strong walls around this stuff and as long as I stayed in the United States the walls stayed in place. I went overseas and the walls were provided by the society [of the UAE]. When I came back they were no longer adequate and I fell apart.

When I went to the United Arab Emirates, safety for women was an absolute. Arab society was built on the fact that men can't control their impulses, that men will steal women for their own use, that women have to be concealed and protected. As a Westerner I didn't have to be concealed or accompanied by a male relative whenever I left my home. Other Arab countries required that, but the UAE didn't. What they did have was built-in protection. I remember the large, walled, protected women and children's parks where no male over 12 was allowed. We would play and the women would sometimes get together and dance the exotic/erotic belly dance. Laughter. Freedom. Safety. I remember the lines at the DMV and the post office that were for women only. As a Westerner and, even more than that, as an American, I had higher status than anyone except the locals, and attacks on us were simply not tolerated. None of the other ex-patriate groups could get away with ill-treatment of us. The law was not to be played with. Offenses were punished swiftly and surely if you offended one of higher status.

A white Western woman was raped while I was there, and it was like a bank had been robbed or the President's daughter kidnapped. They pulled out all the stops, brought out the dogs, and found the person who had done it. It was just not acceptable there. Maybe that is what it is like to be rich and have high status in this country; maybe the police do work for you then.

I do not trust the police here.

I didn't realize the difference in my defenses until I returned to the States for a few months. I felt like I held my breath while I was here, just waiting for an attack. I didn't really relax until I got back "home" to the UAE. I wanted to stay there forever.

I didn't get to. There really was no solution to my son's schooling problem. He was in special ed classes, and the school that had provided that service discontinued it. I couldn't bring myself to send him to a boarding school. The option other ex-pat groups used, sending older children back to the home country to live with their extended families, isn't the American way. So I had to move back.

I remember thinking that it was Michigan that was the problem, that it would be different elsewhere. So when we came back we moved to Arizona. I wanted to stay in the desert. I cried most of the trip back to the US. There were so many things that I loved about being in the UAE.

The lack of safety was what horrified me as soon as I got to Arizona. There were road rage shootings, and in Arizona they might shoot back. It was like being in the Wild West. I called a friend still in the UAE, telling him about the daily murders in the area, the "war zone" mentality that people lived with. My sister [Betty] in Ohio sent me a message – get some mace and keep it with you.

I couldn't figure out how to live like everyone else was living. I tried talking to people. In what I now recognize as typical American style, they refused to believe that any place is really any different than any other. I went to the Catholic Church, looking for the openness and community I had found in the UAE. My smiling openness was met with suspicion, even in the pew, even as we exchanged the "sign of peace." No longer could I drive with my window open, singing with the music, maybe even dancing a little to it, and be met by smiles from other drivers and newspaper sellers. They came out and said it. "Do not make eye contact with other drivers, for you may become a target." Why were these people living like this?

And why couldn't I? I didn't fit; the protection I had in the UAE wasn't there, though I didn't think of it in those terms. I just knew I did not like it.

We moved to Arizona in August. The seizures started in April of the next year, 1994. It is now 2005, and they haven't stopped.

I didn't know what was going on, so I paid attention to the professionals around me. It was stress, it was moving too much, it was coming to Arizona with no support. It was boundary issues. No one believed that things had been different elsewhere. I couldn't stop my body from jerking, first just my right arm and then, as time went on, everything but my trunk would jerk. I didn't lose consciousness, but I would shake and jerk for an hour or more at a time. I was exhausted most of the time, tired for days after a violent one, tired for days from the drugs that were supposed to prevent it.

I switched jobs, from teaching high school to one with less stress. I did yoga and swam. I followed people's advice and read books and talked to doctors and counselors. Their solutions weren't enough for me to work full time. From being a shining star, an organizer, a lead teacher who wrote curriculum in the UAE, from being a member of the Parish Council and leader of the children's choir, I became a person who couldn't be trusted to get her minimal bookkeeping done, who couldn't show up for practices and even be a member of the choir, a person who was of little use.

O my strong little girl, where did you go?

Sunday, March 13

6:30 a.m.

Yesterday was a day of rest.

I tried to talk to Cathy [my sponsor] about the last session, the joy that I was only raped and not killed. She didn't get it. The rape was the most important thing to her. That's what other people said, and I paid too much attention to them. I know now that the really important thing was that I escaped from being murdered.

The idea that things freeze and can be re-experienced again and again must be understood if anyone is to understand what is happening to me, and what I now know happens to other people. It is not just that horrible things happen to you. Sure, that is bad; people should try to do everything they can to prevent others from going through horrible things, from being subjected to horrible things. But for me and for many others, emotionally, those horrible things do not stop; these events feel part of our current lives. It is not sufficient to convince my mind that it is over and past; it is not sufficient to convince my mind that others agree it was a horrible thing

These memories of terror are like a roller coaster ride, and the terror and screams when you go upside down for that split second. What if there was a part of you that knew you were back on safe ground, but another part of you stayed upside down and kept screaming?

You would silence the part of you that said it wasn't over. You would tell others about the ride, and they would affirm that the ride was over. The part of you that was stuck wouldn't get unstuck because of all these words and the fact that it was over. My own response to my stuck part was to tell myself to just stop it and, if you can't, then ignore it.

The EMDR process is going back to get whatever part of me is stuck there, to relive it without denial. Then I understand it is a memory and is in the past.

It seems to me very important that others know this. I believe that well-meaning people, or paid professionals, regardless of their intentions, do very harmful things when they consistently define our lives for us. I know there are times when we pick up things in our past to make ourselves feel worse. That is part of the fourth and fifth steps of recovery, finding the bag of old things we use to feel sorry for ourselves and continue drinking. It is enough to understand, it does get better.

But when you are stuck, you need to go there to finish it, go to where you became overloaded and a part of you just stopped living. What has to happen and is happening is that I have to go even deeper into that time and find that part.

I replay conversations I've had with therapists and others about therapy. "But you know that is over, you know that he or she was sick, just move on with your life" is a supreme denial of that whole part of yourself that didn't make it through the moment. As I go back I can comfort that stuck part, I can understand it and admire that part of me that everyone, including myself, has denied and hidden.

I still do not want to go out much or interact with other people. I want to be in my mind looking around, or resting from all the looking. I don't really want to call someone to work for me tomorrow. Why am I so hesitant to pick up the phone? They may ask what is wrong, and I do not want their opinions. I don't want to try to tell them what is going on with me. I suppose I can just say I need someone to work for me. That will work.

I feel very free as I think of having more days before I have to spend hours pretending that the world is not changing around me.

Monday, March 14

3:30 p.m.

I didn't go to work today but went to a [12-step] meeting. I have been thinking that the seizures are tied up with these frozen memories, but it was the fan that did it in the meeting. It wasn't too bad at first. The fan was going pretty fast and it was loud so I turned it off. At least, I thought I did. But it kept going – the fan with the light behind it, the shadows, the constant barely-perceived flick-flick of the light. I didn't notice it right away, but my body noticed and started shaking a little. By the time I was conscious of it, it was too late for me to try to find the right switch. I asked someone sitting there if he could find out how to turn it off, but he couldn't, so I left the meeting. I got to a table and got my glasses off and safe just in time – one of the wild head seizures, hair flying. Someone was suggesting calling an ambulance when two people from the meeting got there and calmed the ones thinking about the ambulance. Someone had an arm around me, talking softly and telling me to take deep breaths. I could feel the tension leave and got calm enough to go back into the meeting. Someone had turned off the fan.

I feel it in my body, like once when I was really high and the feel of the black light was too much for me to take. If there is no physical reason for the reaction, maybe it is a memory. I don't get resonance within me when I think of flicking lights flicking and flicking. Bright lights overhead in the stores also cause me to have seizures.

I had been trying to travel the road that says this is about emotions redirected to the body, that it is a problem of how I handle my emotions right now. That [belief] is leaving, along with the belief that I am a target and evil people can somehow sense me. I don't believe that, but I still have seizures and don't want to go out a lot.

I think there is still a lot that needs the revisiting that EMDR does, maybe on why I think I'm not good enough for nice things. What's that about? At a rummage sale I keep going for the older things, the battered things, the things that others do not want. I went to a hardware store and bought a bottle of old nails and screws when I moved in here. Why not new nails? I have gotten some boxes of new nails, but I look around for the bottle of rusted nails. I notice strange things like that, like noticing myself wringing my hands. I can be sitting at the table thinking and notice my hands doing this strange dance around each other.

Maybe my part is to keep noticing things, keep track of things like I once tracked every seizure. Maybe I ignore my feelings.

Sometimes I feel so lost. And then I cut down on the things I am doing, cut down on the number of decisions I will make today, on the number of things I will expect of myself today. I cut down on my life.

Tuesday, March 15

10:00 a.m.

Just got home from a meeting, a beginner's meeting, the first three steps. I talked about how hard life had to become to convince me that my life had become unmanageable. It seemed anything could happen to me and I still wouldn't admit it was out of control. How I could be beaten up and raped, my life could be threatened, I could be held hostage all night by an insane person, and that still wasn't enough. It took waking up in the morning to find my five-month-old baby's diaper was muddy and I didn't know where he had been. That was what it took for me to realize that I was powerless.

Also in my mind was a news story about a woman in Atlanta who was kidnapped by a man who had escaped from the courthouse, who had already killed three people. He kept her in her condo all night. She lived through it. She made him pancakes. I thought about writing her a letter and telling her how wonderful it was that she made it, and how smart she was, and how it was now okay for her to cry.

And I started crying, little tears seeping out all meeting. I was so very sad about what happened to me happening to that woman in Atlanta. I looked around the room and picked people that I wanted to talk to. One of them was a man whom I have known for 17 years. You get really close to people when you see them even once a week for years on end, and talk about the reality of your life and how you are making it through one day at a time. He is a very special person. The other person was a woman who is really new. I talked to her last night, and we had planned to talk after the meeting about getting over the pride and independence that keeps us from asking for help. She could be part of this.

I sat them down and just talked about it, just talked about what had happened with Preacher, told them the story and cried. The man in particular wanted to jump to the rape as the bad thing (men are getting so much better about rape being a bad thing), but I didn't let him go there. The rape was the victory! But unlike the other night with Nova, where we ended with celebrating the joy that I felt when I knew I was just going to be raped, that I was not going to be beheaded, I cried today because it is sad that I had to live through it. I talked about frozen memory, and I heard my voice and felt my face getting weird as I went through it. They noticed when I finished and when my face and voice changed back.

I don't know if I am finished crying about it [the Preacher incident]. During it, I never had time to feel sad. I had to keep my emotions totally in check because my life depended on it. Afterward I was so busy with moving, opening the new office, finding my way in a new city and then dealing with the pregnancy. My life was too busy to feel sad about it.

Wednesday, March 16

10:30 a.m.

The Preacher thing is going back to where it should be. It is not all the way there, but it is certainly moving. There is still some sadness. I can feel it welling up at this moment, but there is a definite flavor of saying goodbye. Maybe I'll never finish with all the sadness. Maybe I need to work more on this with Nova in the next session. It's not as gone as the whole Alex thing.

The process is continuing. I'm feeling much more competent, both yesterday and today, more able to make decisions, deal with the world, and handle the tasks in front of me. I'm making progress.

Thursday, March 17

7:45 p.m.

The day has gone by too quickly it seems. There has been sadness with me most of the day. I got some pictures from my sister Betty. The Christmas after Dad moved out of the house, I wrote 50 pages of memories about our times there. Betty sent me the pictures that went with it, plus some more of the family; I printed what I had written and read it several times. Good things, but also Mom and Chuck's deaths, two weeks apart. Lots of sadness still there. My head is shaking some now. My right hand was going for a while today. I haven't called anyone to work for me tomorrow, but I don't want to go. I may have a session with Nova tomorrow night. I have phone calls to make and don't really want to make them. But I will just relax for a while, stop the shaking, and get it done.

Friday, March 18

7:10 a.m.

I went to bed last night planning on going to work today. As the time nears to leave, there is a little voice inside me saying *no, don't go there!*

I have a choice to say shut up I'm going or to say why do you not want to go? When I go with the latter, my face and mouth change. I frown and my lips come out in a pout.

I want to stay here and play. I am so tired of working all the time.

My little girl doesn't want to do this. I cry and rock as I write this. Poor little girl, you will be okay. Mama loves you. Don't worry so much. I won't make you go. And I can feel her leave. She is happy because she got her way. I ask her if it is just to get her way and she comes back with the frown and the pout. She is quite clear.

It is not that I don't want to work ever; it is just that it was too much. I was so very tired all the time.

Good little Catholic girl, you are allowed to rest. Then you can work again. You are strong, but sometimes you need to rest. You do lots of good work, but it is okay for you to take a break. Everyone needs a break.

Mama needed lots of breaks, but she never got them. She worked too much, too much, all the time. Poor Mama. With all those kids. Poor little mama.

But little girl, she must have been happy with Daddy or she wouldn't have had so many babies! There were times of joy for her; there must have been. There were later, for sure, but not enough when we were all there. Not enough for Mama, not enough for the little girl watching Mama.

Only one time I remember sitting on her lap, reading my very first words about David and Ann and their slide. She laughed at that, she laughed when I could read. I liked it so much when my mama could laugh. It didn't happen enough for me; it didn't happen enough because of me. I can make people laugh now, Mama, I can do that now, but I couldn't do that with you. I'm sorry, Mama. I wish I could have made things better for you, easier for you, but I tried my best. I was your best little trier, I was. I loved you a lot; you were always the best in the whole world. There was never a Mama better than you. You worked so much.

Daddy is doing okay now, Mama. He is fine. He has a lady that he takes care of, and it is funny. It is like watching him with Aunt Gladys, his aunt. She would say, "Johnny, go get me this!" and Daddy would get up and run like a little boy. He would say, "Yes, ma'am" in his softer, younger voice. Ethel is like that. She can't see, Mama; she lost most of her sight and it is too bad. Sometimes she gets mad about it at Daddy. She doesn't have good kids; they don't take care of her at all. But Daddy does; he is good. He takes her places and visits with her, and sometimes lets her get away with putting down the wrong card. Not very much; you know how Daddy is with cards. There, you laughed! I can hear you laugh, I can see you smile. I miss you, Mama. I wish you had gotten to stay here longer.

It is sad without you. Betty has taken your role, kind of. Can you believe it? Betty who was so bad at things around the house, who was just one of the little ones. She calls everyone, and passes on the news, and tells you when it has been too long since you have been home. Maybe you were like Betty. Maybe you liked to stay at home a lot. There was a wonderful thing in Chicago, a wonderful painter with pictures that make your mind get big and the world fill up with color. But Betty didn't want to go; she wanted to stay home. I hope there was some of that in you, Mama. I hope that mostly you liked to stay home with all your kids around you. Maybe it was good for you to have a swarm of little people on you, around you, with you. Maybe it was not all hard, hard work to you.

You can stay home, little girl. Stay home from work, and we will go to the meeting where the people like you and you get lots of hugs. You will like it; it will be good for you. I will call the man at work and tell him no, I am not coming today. Maybe another day. You can stay out and play now.

SESSION FOUR

Saturday, March 19

We didn't do any of the EMDR last night. I read a lot. I read the journal [entries] to Nova. There is no doubt that the incident with Alex is done. The incident with Preacher is moving there. My story, my perceptions, are valid and I paid too much attention to other people. I don't have to do that. That is important for me to remember, to keep telling myself.

I read the part that I wrote about therapists and their tendency to tell us, to become the experts in interpreting one's own life. They often seem to decide what the truth is for someone else. I let someone else deny my own reality. Nova said she had talked of that when she was learning to become a therapist, how dangerous it was for the client and so tempting for the therapist. How her professor warned her about getting kicked out of school for that heresy, though he didn't call it that.

I read the memory book that I did for my family to Nova last night. Dad moved from the house we grew up in and I wrote the house memories booklet in 1997. I went through each room of the house and talked about special times there. It seems to have happened years ago. When I read it to Nova, I felt some distance from it. Not like the day before when I had first read, then re-read it; I felt it all then. Things were now falling into place, into a truer place.

I've always thought we were rather Waltonesque [like the family in the seventies TV show]. We were so very stable, so involved with each other, so part of each other. There is a push on TV for the family table, trying to get people to sit with their family and eat dinner together one night a week. In my house, we did that every day, same time, same places at the table. A sameness and a security. The slowness of time passing there. The things that were worth noting when I wrote that [memory book], the very simple things that resonated with my brothers and sisters when they read it. The flood of memories that were shared. If we would have done EMDR, it would have been on the deaths of my mother and my brother Chuck, only two weeks apart. I wrote about all of us sitting around the dining room table, waiting to hear if the dental records matched, if indeed it was my brother Chuck who had burned to death in his house. He has. Still a lot of sadness about that time.

The things all of that brought back. A lot about Mom. I know how I felt about her life; I know how much I hated the thought of that life for me. But from her point of view, was it all that bad? Could she have liked the way the kids clustered about her, how many of them there were? The laughter really was there for her at times. I was a child looking at her, and didn't really get to know her as an adult. She was still alive when my son Jon was born, though gone before he turned two. She came up to Michigan to help me right after the birth, stayed for two weeks, I think. I was amazed at how much trouble it is to take care of an infant and asked her how she did it with six of them. She said she thought she was just insane during those years. I realize that was her life, and her choices, and that I know very little about it. I did the best I could, and I think it [my guilt] may be over.

NOVA'S COMMENTS ON SESSION FOUR

When Mary first read me her description of her family home and her Christmas present to her brothers and sisters in 1997 when her father finally moved from the house, I was overwhelmed by the perfection of this family scene. It was the way we all were supposed to be brought up – close, loving, enjoying each other and enjoying innocent family entertainments together. These were "the olden days," the golden days that are a reproach to each new generation. How could Mary have gone from this family into some of the horrendous situations and dangers she has described to me? The upbringing she described should have lent protection even for one living through the Hippie Age. As her story unfolded, the contradictions disappeared.

INTERVAL FOUR

Saturday, March 19

7:30 a.m

I had to come here fast, to write this down quickly, before I lose it. I just thought of the timing.

1976   Alex, Preacher, and another dangerous incident
1977   Jon is born, I get sober
1978   Mom and Chuck die

Three years. It was only three years, and all that happened. I have never really looked at that. Three years. Not much time at all. It all happened in three years.

My mind is reeling from the reality. Much like the three incidents in 1976 took years in my mind, were unconnected to the flow of events as [they] are normally measured, I have never realized how they all hit me so quickly. No wonder I never fully felt through them.

Rob once talked to me about making the things in your life into a story. He was cautioning me about our relationship, that I could make it into a tragedy if I wanted. That would be sad, that would be untrue, and that would have prevented us from being friends.

1977 is a story year, getting sober and the things with Jonathan that led up to getting sober. It is a story that I tell on a regular basis, for it is the story that, if I forget, I may drink again. Part of 1976 fits into that story; it is from there that I draw the things that I don't have to do anymore, and it is only last week that it grew to include the time with Preacher as what it was. It is only since I've started this journey that 1976 became a year instead of a hundred years. 1978 was a year in sobriety, in my mind eons later than 1977.

Fitting in here is what happened after the therapy. The woman whom I had sit with me while I told the story of Preacher and cried last week called me last night. She told me her story of being attacked and threatened with a knife, and how she is still afraid over 15 years later. [details deleted for privacy] How she thinks this EMDR stuff might work for her.

I want to wave my fingers and make her better

Sunday, March 20

6:00 p.m.

I decided to not work for at least the next three weeks, maybe the rest of the semester, and just go to the 8:15 am [12-step] meeting. So I called and got a sub for Mondays for the next three weeks, and will do the same for Friday. I don't want to be distracted by work.

I am feeling much more confident. I'm having a good time getting reacquainted with all of me. Both my little girl and my big girl don't want to go to work, so I will stay here, and rearrange my house, listen to music, go out when I want to, stay in when I want, and get better.

Monday, March 21

10:30 a.m.

It seems that my house is much bigger, that I am taking over my house for my use. It is strange; I am taller, and my house is bigger. I plan on going through things and getting rid of the stuff my son and his family have stored here, stuff my last boyfriend left, unknown stuff. I want to use this space for me, for what I want right now, and that feels good. It's like I just moved in. I can take the space around me for myself; I can let it be mine.

This journal is important to me. My memory is not good, especially when one day is separate and different from the next. I need this to track my journey, and it was scary this morning when I thought I lost yesterday's entry. I need to run a hard copy for backup.

Tuesday, March 22

10:15 a.m.

I really hate confrontations with people. I can feel the tension from this encounter in my body, revving up, wanting to seize. It is strange. Sometimes it is okay to confront someone; there is no tension. Other times, most times, there is tension. It's high today because of the backlog. Two things under warranty need to be fixed, always a hassle. Tension from the new computer, trying to get things set up, trying not to inadvertently sign up for things I don't want to pay for. And the head is starting to shake as I write. But at least I have my CD player; I can play music and chill.

Taking over my house means to me having those places, those things, that help me chill available easily. Like the online game, like the music. I'm going to work on my room today, have a serene place for me.

And just thinking about it all and the other tasks I have to do is keeping the head moving.

Time for music, some breakfast, and chilling.

Wednesday, March 23

10:00 a.m.

I feel like I'm redefining myself to myself. There is still a voice in me that says, Who are you to be doing …? whatever. This morning, it is not so very loud, but I am aware of it. I talked to someone about running for the Board at the club [which provides rooms for meetings], and also got fired as her [12-step] sponsor by a woman whom I advised not to run. The murmur underneath is about who am I to even think about this stuff. It's not loud enough for me to really hear. I know I've identified it as male before, but right now I don't have a clue about it.

Resistance to going there translates into some shakiness in the body. I think that is true. If I follow it farther, I hit sadness, and I don't want to be sad. Who is sad in there and why? Is it my little girl? No, she's looking at someone else, some other part of me. A bigger girl, maybe even a young woman. I can feel the override kick in, the "that is not true, don't even go there" idea. The "we have things to do, don't worry about that" thing. The avoidance that has become a hindrance, even if at one point it helped me make it through the night. It doesn't do that now.

Zeroing in on something. I'll just have to let it come.

Thursday, March 24

10:20 a.m.

I feel pretty far away from all the commotion that has been going on inside me right now. Tonight is my next session. I want to finish the last of the horrors, though it has been diminishing as time has gone on. I don't know what to expect; it may be contributing to my feeling of being totally under attack by the modern world. Like the modern world got filed wrong or something, got filed in with the fear that "they" can sense me. I know in my mind that the greed [of businesses in this country] is there for all people, that businesses are certainly not focused just on me, but on everyone. My hope is that tonight will shake that connection up somehow. So much has already happened, but I know there is more to come, more to do, more to look at.

The voice that lurks, that I can see out of the corner of my conscious mind. I know that EMDR will help bring it into focus when the time is right. But not tonight; tonight it will be the Walter thing, the mixture of date rape and gang rape. Already it feels like an old, boring story. But I want to be sure it is gone and not just resting somewhere. I'm ready, my little girl is ready, and I already took tomorrow and the next two weeks off. Primed and ready to go.

SESSION FIVE

Thursday, March 24

The EMDR session tonight was on the gang rape at Walter's house, when his friends and brother raped me while Walter was there. I never liked Walter much. We didn't click in any way, but I couldn't see any reason not to see him. Phyllis was dating one of his brothers, and my dating Walter made that relationship stronger. Maybe it was just pity dates; I don't know. But I felt in some way to blame.

Start of Session

Negative Cognition: I was guilty in some way for causing this. Level of belief: fairly strong belief that it was my fault.

Positive Cognition: It was not my fault at all. Level of belief: I almost totally disbelieve that.

Nova waved her fingers, I followed with my eyes, and I remembered.

It seemed to start with putting it [the incident] into time. It was before Alex, right after Ora and I moved to the house on the little dead-end street. I know because I remembered seeing Walter and his brother at Phyllis's house on the south side, which was usually where I saw him. He had not been to the new house before; it was just after we moved there. This is new; these three terror incidents were not tied to dates before! Anyway, Walter had picked me up somewhere else. We went to his house, drank for a while, took some acid, and ended up in his bed. I hadn't gotten off on the acid yet. We'd had sex and he left the room supposedly to get something to drink.

Next thing I know some other guys come in, just one at first, then a couple more. I pull up the sheets and tell them to get out, what do they think they are doing? They made it pretty clear what they wanted to do. One of them joined me on the bed, then another. I was hollering for Walter and yelling at them when one of them, Walter's brother Ernest, put his hand around my neck and pressed my windpipe with his fingers. I couldn't breathe, didn't think I would ever breathe again. "Shut up and do it," he said. So I did.

I don't remember the sequence of events. I know that at one point I had three of them on me at once, someone riding my mouth while someone else was on my breasts, another one just fucking me. At one point Walter came in, and I asked him for help, screamed at him to help. I don't recall him saying anything. I don't know how long it went on. There were five all told, so must have been four of them that were on me then. Walter didn't join the gang.

One of them, the largest one in terms of size, was called Hawk. He seemed sad; he wasn't really into it. He seemed to be the nice one.

When they were all through, they left Walter and me alone. I begged him to let me go, told him that I wouldn't tell anyone, that all I wanted to do was get away. Just let me out of the house. But don't leave me alone with Ernest, he's crazy.

I get dressed and Walter and I go out to his car. Ernest joined us and Walter left. Ernest told me he would just as soon kill me, but he wouldn't if I didn't tell anyone. Walter came back, Ernest left, and for some reason Walter took me to one of his other brothers' house, the one that Phyllis was dating. He asked his brother if he wanted some of me, but the brother said no. I tried to get help from that brother, to get him to make Walter let me go, but he wasn't interested in me. As I think of it now, I don't know if Walter did anything else to me; he may have. Finally, he decided to take me home.

He didn't know where the new house was, so I had him drop me off blocks away, and I just took off running, through back yards so they couldn't see where I went. I don't know who was with Walter at that point; I just know there were two of them in the car.

When I got home, Phyllis and Ora were there. They didn't believe me. I don't know why. I guess Phyllis didn't want to know anything bad about that family.

I didn't realize until tonight that Walter must have set this thing up! That was the biggest surprise, the thing I hadn't known before.

At that point in my life I was drinking really heavily and frequently blacked out. We [Walter and I] had talked about that while we were drinking that night, even, and had talked about it before. I know he was around during my one month of sobriety. I had gone to a psychologist about my "recurrent amnesia" and had proved I wasn't an alcoholic by staying sober for a month. Did a lot of drugs, but didn't drink. I hated it! Anyway, she [the psychologist] decided I was a manic-depressive and gave me drugs. I didn't mind that!

Walter was around during that [month of sobriety]. He didn't like me any more than I liked him. He picked me out as a drunken white girl who had memory loss and set me up. While Ernest had the reputation of being the crazy one of the brothers (I think there were five of them, and pretty powerful in the community), Walter is the one that was found, bloody and wandering down the highway. The police picked him up and took him back to his car, where they found his three children and maybe his wife, all dead. Walter said he didn't know what had happened, but he did time for it. [I don't remember when I found out about that or when that was.]

He was just a predator, looking for someone, and I was that someone. It was an incident in time. It took place during what was a really hard year, did in fact start that very hard year or nine months or whatever that encompass the entire horror time. It is amazing that only a short time ago I thought they were all spread out over years. Even now, I need to look at a list on the paper to keep the idea from running out of my mind.

I had already gotten rid of the "black hole pulling me in" idea, the "they can smell my fear and so they come" notion. What I got rid of tonight was that my "pity date attitude" had anything to do with the event. He never connected with me in any way, never enough to pick that up. He was looking for someone for some "fun" and found me.

End of Session

Negative Cognition: I was guilty in some way for causing this. Level of belief: do not believe it at all

Positive Cognition: It was not my fault at all. Level of belief: totally believe that statement

We [Nova and I] ended up talking about how I ran into Hawk one day while I was handing out leaflets at the GM plant. I gave him one and then noticed who he was. It seemed funny to think about the "correct" way to handle that. "Excuse me, haven't I met you before? Weren't you at a rape with me?" Nova and I laughed about that.

NOVA'S COMMENTS ON SESSION FIVE

Again in this session, when Mary remembered the event during EMDR, she was able to understand the attitudes and motives of the participants much better than she had in the past. For years she had thought of Walter as someone who liked her and toward whom she was rather indifferent. She felt guilty toward him because she was dating him to help her friend stay friendly with his brother. She didn't blame him for the gang rape. She thought it just happened. She thought he should have interfered and helped her more than he did, but it had never occurred to her before that he arranged the whole thing. As she stated, she saw for the first time that, instead of being a young lovesick boy she was using, he was indifferent to her as a person. He saw himself as a predator and her as simple and available prey. Mary had never really understood the jungle in which she was living.

INTERVAL FIVE

Friday, March 25

10:10 a.m.

    I am reclaiming my hippie persona! I'm listening to the *Woodstock* CD, to Jefferson Airplane singing "Volunteers." "It's a new dawn!" Go, Gracie! I can't believe how happy I am today. Filled with joy. It's incredible and inexplicable.

    My emotions are all over. I sat and cried for a while at the meeting this morning, as inexplicable as the rushes of joy. My mind is filled with the image of me as a hippie, me in a long, flowered dress and a beaded necklace, in a sunny field with the sun in my smile. While I am by myself in this vision, I know that there are many people near that are part of me in some way. Those times were wonderful while they lasted.

    Acid. I don't think I ever got off on the acid that Walter gave me that night. The roach that I was sure was in the Kool-Aid at home once I got there afterwards might have been a hallucination, might have been part of why Ora and Phyllis didn't believe me.

    Life didn't end well for many of those people I first met in my hippie days. [My ex] Tommy Walker died in prison from complications of diabetes that would have been treated differently if he was out. Greg P., Tommy's best friend, had been killed in prison. Raymond, Tommy's brother, Beth's father, got lost in coke for a while and died from complications of diabetes. Another friend, Gene, supposedly killed himself playing Russian roulette. He was such a joyful man. I hardly ever saw him without his guitar; he was always making music and bringing carloads of hungry people to my house. I think he was probably killed because he played with the big guys, running drugs and guns on the Detroit-Chicago route, and couldn't leave the little girls alone. He never met a teenage white girl that he didn't love, and playing there [being distracted by girls who didn't understand how serious his time commitments were] and not attending to business is what I think it was. It turned bad.

For a while, it was wonderful, but the price that was paid by many was really high. Life was intense then, wonderful or horrible, and missed a lot of middle parts. We were all connected with each other and the universe. That was what it felt like to me. That we could love each other, and take care of each other, and we would all make it through, would all be okay. Tragically wrong in the long term, incredibly wonderful in the short term.

As I think about it now, I assumed everyone was where I was but they weren't. Bob didn't feel loved enough. Phyllis misses the drugs more than anything else. More than the community. She said, "Kids today just don't know what being really high is." High and exploring the world, high and looking at the world like a child, seeing the wonder and the beauty around me and the specialness of all individuals. It really did feel like I loved everyone and everyone loved me.

I have been afraid of night. [I didn't used to be afraid.] My strong girl singing at the top of my voice, walking to get my sister. My hippie girl, wandering with my love, owning the night, part of the night, loving its shadows and the room that was there. Part of it, enjoying it. I have been afraid of it for so long, and as I look for the fear at this moment, I notice that some of it is gone.

I need to find some of my women's music, the stuff that was a source of life when I was in the UAE, affirming who I am, talking of power. "Take back the night" on a personal level. That is one of the goals of my whole journey right now, that things will connect and I can be alive outside in the night. To go sing somewhere, to take a walk, to drive wherever I want. I love night driving on empty roads, driving to meet the dawn.

Saturday, March 26

9:10 a.m.

I think we are losing this morning; my strong girl, my hippie girl, we are not doing very well. I've been thinking, and it seems that when you have sex with lots of people, no one thinks you have the right to say no.

I'm not real sure how I got there. I know at one point I really liked all the men I slept with, I could think of them and feel warm, know things that were exclusively theirs, how they were special. Somewhere along the line that changed. It was only people I really didn't like for some big reason that I wouldn't sleep with. Sometimes I think I turned into an animal when I was drunk. So very much of my life was at the unconscious level.

I had been involved in lots of different sexual scenarios; lots of fantasies got played out with me as part of them. I think that is why Phyllis and Ora didn't react to the gang rape. Somehow even the women thought I had lost the right to say no, since I so rarely used it.

I am very sad and scared, and I don't want to go outside at all. There's a little conversation going on inside of me, with a calm part trying to convince me that I can go work in the yard. I like working in the yard and may do that. The other part of me really resists the idea. I will have to fight that resistance to actually step outside. I wonder if I will win.

I am sad today about my son Jon. I took him to a job interview yesterday at Arby's. He is so lost. He seems to have little energy for anything; the house he lives in is a pit. His speech is getting sloppier. He had so many years of speech therapy, but he still has to think about it to speak clearly. He couldn't remember where the Arby's was and had to call his ex-wife and ask her.

I'm not as scared about myself. If I don't have a job at the college anymore, I'll just find something else. I only need to make a couple of hundred dollars for ends to meet.

But my mind is still wandering – my relationships with my Dad, my boss, Ora B, all are rushing through my mind, sparking more and more questions I don't know the answers to.

Sunday, March 27

1:45 p.m.

Yesterday turned into quite a bad day. I didn't even get dressed or go out of the house. I cleaned a little. The house looks more austere every day and I really like it. Played a computer game. Slept. Thought about rearranging things. Read. Fairly depressed, I guess. Didn't talk to anyone I didn't want to. I like caller ID!

I got up really early this morning, feeling sad about my life. I thought about writing about it, but didn't want to. Just played some more, and now I find I am in a different spot. Didn't like my morning [12-step] meeting. A woman who fired me as her sponsor sat next to me, and I just didn't like being close to her. Started seizing, softly, then harder. Had to get a ride home, but luckily the guys were there who bring my car home when they bring me. That is always nice.

As I started feeling better, I really looked at myself and was quite shocked. I have gotten old! And very large. I haven't been taking care of my poor little body. I'm thinking about treating myself to a nice life. That means not spending time with people I don't like and don't want to be with. Not spending time doing things that I don't really want to do.

The sun is shining and the birds are singing. Maybe I'll just live in my neighborhood all summer. Retire the car, walk where I want to. Explore the neighborhood; it's really quite nice.

What a nice dream of my summer! I will play in the yard and do yoga in my bedroom. I might even paint my garage and my fence! It will be a beautiful place, and I won't even let the bad people in, the bad attitudes in. I will figure out how I can be me and I can make them leave me alone. I don't know if I can do that with all of them in my face all the time. Just like I pretended all those houses weren't there, that it was just a big forest with a few houses like when I was pregnant, I will just make this my "place to get better." Last year, my goal was to be able to dance all night when my son got married, and I did it. This year I will be able to run by the end of the summer, just run run run for the sheer pleasure of it. I will live today like that is what is going to happen.

Today I will not think about doing anything except what I talked about above. Live in a dream of the summer that may or may not be possible, but oh, it sounds so very nice.

Monday, March 28

5:15 a.m.

Yesterday turned out to be a good day, and today is looking good already. In this process I have gotten taller, my house has become larger and totally mine, and now I think I'm reclaiming my body. There is no resistance this moment to moving, to walking around the block in the dark, to doing some yoga, no murmurs from within, no dread, no voice saying "you have to not move". Was that really what that wordless dread was saying? "Don't move, they won't see you if you don't move"? How very strange.

Today I will spend like yesterday, not letting the mean people into my life. I do not have to talk to people who bore me or appall me or are rude. I may just quit the Sunday meeting. Why have I been paying so much attention to what other people say? The [12-Step] program rule is we don't have to like you but we have to love you. When asked for help, you give it.

Well, that is nuts. There are limits. It amazes me that I spent a moment of time with this one woman I didn't even like. She was so totally into herself, one of the whiny ones. I couldn't believe it when she asked me to sponsor her, but I kept an open mind and told myself I might learn something. Yeah, I learned what a nasty person she is! And how much she doesn't listen to anyone else's opinion if it doesn't agree with hers. When she fired me [as her sponsor] she told me that I didn't seem to realize how much she has grown, what a beautiful woman she has become. God led her there. God is her justification for whatever she wants to do. Who am I to tell her anything when God is revealing himself to her? What nonsense.

There are limits. I'm not hiding from anyone. I'm not isolating. I'm just going to keep the people I don't want in my life out of my life. What was I thinking? I think I had lost faith in myself. Losing control of my body seemed to put me in the wrong and shook my idea of myself.

Not today. No doubts for me today. No hiding who I am today.

I wonder if it's too cold to walk around the block.

Tuesday, March 29

9:45 a.m.

Yesterday was a good day, lots of energy, not much resistance to doing things. I managed to be busy all morning, run errands after my nap, and even call my Dad at night. That felt great! I haven't been able to do that much in one day for a while.

I did not do so well this morning. I am pretty sad as I write this, but I don't want to think about why. I want to go play in my yard. I got the things I needed to rake and plant some seeds and even put down some grass seed if I feel like it. And that seems like a great thing to do today. My back yard feels really safe.

Why am I sad? I will spend a minute on that thought before I chase it away. It could be the time I've wasted. It amazes me that my inner landscape has changed so much in the last month, and although it saddens me to think of the years that I spent not knowing this, I'm mostly glad that I have made it this far.

Upset about the world? The consumer culture? The sheer greed around me? Why do I feel like I am being gnawed on by flesh-eaters? And that I am surrounded by folks saying it feels good to be eaten that way?

But I am not going there today. Goodness knows I am changing so much that I don't know where I will be when I have to make decisions about interacting with the world.

I'll think about it if I want to while I play in my yard.

Wednesday, March 30

7:00 a.m.

excerpt from an email to Bob

It is interesting to get your take on my journals. You are very sweet, and very supportive. It is nice to have my words acknowledged, and my journey followed.

I'm going places in my head where all kinds of things are stored that I have denied myself access to. It is very interesting. One of the best things about EMDR is that I am not afraid when I go there.

The other day I said something about being old and fat. Wow, the limits of language. Or my use of it. It is quite wonderful to me to be living again in my whole body as opposed to thinking of myself as hiding out in an armored vehicle, which my body had become. This is finally me! I have been disconnected from my body for a long time. I have ignored it without noticing. That is getting better.

The problem that EMDR has been helping rectify is that horrible incidents in my past have not been located in the place in the brain that stores memories. They have been locked up somewhere, protected and alive and current. Part of the process has been reliving them in a non-painful way and finishing the process of dealing with them. The pain and tears the day or so after a session are good; they are finishing.

Another thing that is incredibly exciting is they are finding their place in time in relation to other things and situations. They are becoming memories. We don't "get over" being 10; we just turn 11. We don't get over the good times we have in the past; they just become more distant. But for me the traumas didn't recede to the past. For me, it was necessary for me to go through the EMDR process to allow my brain to process things in the natural way. I don't have to learn how to let the past be the past; I have to allow my brain to do what it knows how to do.

Friday, April 1

4:45 p.m.

I took yesterday off and didn't write anything, didn't do much at all. It was a wet, dreary day, and I spent most of the day playing on the computer. Today is much better. It is sunny and I feel much more capable. Tonight is the next session. I'm thinking of doing something different, something about how I deal with day-to-day life. I've been reading about dealing with things besides trauma. Maybe one of the times when I just can't seem to leave the house. Maybe we could do the dread thing about going to work. I don't think I'm totally understanding what those things are about; they seem like a strange way to react. The traumatic things that happened to me seem very far away now.

SESSION SIX

Friday, April 1

The session tonight focused on working at the community college. It was a different kind of session, not driven by a trauma but by how much I dread going to work. The dread doesn't make sense. I have to work some to live. My disability isn't that much. It would seem that I would just go in and work. But I feel like I am under attack. That is what we tried to look at.

Start of Session

Negative Cognition: When I go to work, I am going into a hostile environment and I have to be on guard. Belief: highest on scale

Positive Cognition: I can go to work and do my job as best I can and then leave. Belief: lowest on scale

We did many more eye movements than we had done in the past. The scenario was just me going to work. I described the people and places that I see as I get ready to deal with students, and what goes on while I am dealing with students.

It was probably the second time through the scenario that I got really angry and shouted a lot. I am often left to fend for myself in the work area [where we do one-on-one teaching], and the people who are supposed to be there with me are off doing other things for their lecture classes or dealing with their committee work. So my ability to get work done is hampered and I have limited time with students because the people responsible for helping them are gone.

I thought of coming into the [work area] and saw the whole staff as a wild tribe brandishing spears at me. And in the middle of it is my little girl with her dust mop and tin helmet. What a surprise! That was the part of me that was dealing with the situation.

It was a hard situation. I had worked there before [for four years before I went to the UAE] and had recently returned [after 11 years]. Seemingly everything had changed. I hated the changes, hated the fact that no one could even tell me why they were made. And my little girl was the one who tried to deal with it! Brave little girl, but very used to defending one group and letting the rest of the world be enemies. That was pretty clear tonight. Part of the problem I was having was I saw the whole staff as a monolith, and just me and the students on the other side.

As Nova and I worked, as I followed her fingers with my eyes and talked, it became clearer to me that there were individuals there. Some of the staff were difficult, lazy, and not dependable. But there were others committed to helping the students.

I am left tonight with thinking that I can treat the staff the same way I treat my students, as people who are quite different from each other, with different strengths and weaknesses. That there are ways that I can protect myself from all the interruption and failures of others. I can act like an adult. That will be a change!

End of Session

Negative Cognition: When I go to work, I am going into a hostile environment and I have to be on guard. Belief: almost lowest on scale

Positive Cognition: I can go to work and do my job as best I can and then leave. Belief: almost highest on scale.

NOVA'S COMMENTS ON SESSION SIX

After Session Five, Mary wrote about the interval between Hippie Years and the present, the changes in her youthful view of the world as open to change and improvement, and herself as free, brave, and active, to a feeling of danger from the world and herself as a victim, needing to constrict herself to avoid notice from "the bad people." When she began to think about her situation at work, her first image of coping with "the others" involved her brave little girl with her dust mop and tin helmet, a solution at the five-year-old level of understanding, with bad guys and a hero, good and evil battling. During the EMDR analysis of the situation, Mary was able to see differences between the people with whom she worked, able to recognize various shades of competence and interest, even the presence of excellent and dedicated staff. After this session Mary no longer saw her workplace as hostile and dangerous. She had exorcized the demons.

INTERVAL SIX

Saturday, April 2

8:15 p.m.

I am feeling better and worse today. On one hand, I feel like I can go out. But I went out last night, just to the store shopping, and two nights in a row would be a lot. I am also feeling that it has taken me all this time to get to some really trite things, for example, that the people at work are individuals. Of course they are, and intellectually I know that. It's the emotional response, or the subconscious response, that I am looking for. That is the response, the subtext to my life, that has me reeling.

It's like a man who has been kicked over and over and is lying on the ground. People walk by and he doesn't move, expecting to be kicked. I feel like that. Do I think everyone is going to kick me? Not intellectually. I don't even believe emotionally that most of them will kick me. But the idea that there is another kick coming is what I feel.

The theory that the seizures are related to my intellect overriding my emotions may have some validity. I don't know if the two even communicate! Emotionally I feel like I'm going into battle when I go to work. So I just keep up an inner monologue that I'm only going in to help some students, that I can do that and I am good at it, so I can make myself go to work. Will that change since last night? The positive thing I was working towards last night was believing I can stay calm, do my work, and let anything else flow around me. Right now I believe it less than I did at the end of the session. I am really sad and crying as I write this. I am tired of thinking about it.

Monday, April 4

2:20 p.m.

I started to write yesterday and then just deleted it all, but what I have to write today is just the same, just as humiliating as it was then. I have been in touch with my little girl. What I have been borrowing from her is her black-and-white attitude, that you are either for me or against me. It's a very egocentric view, but how else can I see the thing about work when I have a clear vision of her with her giant dust mop and the staff looking like barbarians with spears? That worked, but it is not the best I can do now. I have to change, which means I have to look clearly at the past. That hurts.

I was not completely wrong, but [my little girl] was really young and didn't understand many things. It is not true that everyone is either for me and mine or against us. Many just don't care. It is not the defining thing in history, me and mine. There really isn't one thing but lots of different things.

I feel stupid missing that. Many of the people at work don't care at all about me one way or the other, have no opinion about me. It was nuts to act like they did. To feel like they did. We can't really control our feelings, though, so I should let up on myself. But I'm not real good at that.

My past is still becoming my past. The integration is still going on.

Wednesday, April 6

10:30 a.m.

The thought of going to work on Monday makes me want to cry. I'm not ready. I feel stupid and incompetent. The last EMDR dealt with anger, and I am not so angry at them, but at myself. My disappointment in myself is coming to the fore, and I need to deal with that. The alternative is to stuff it and go for it, but that has been nonproductive in the past

I am beginning to see that getting myself armed and ready for work takes an incredible amount of energy, and not doing that means that I have time and energy to do other things. I can do the yoga, take walks. I got some things in to be fixed that have been needing fixing for a while, like the screen that was slashed two years ago. I've been attacking the "clutter" in my house. I've been feeling more like I have the energy and time to do things.

It is possible that I can get to the point where going to work is not going to take so much energy, but I don't think that will come about if I go back and use the same tactics that I have been using and want to stop using. So I am going to take the rest of the term off.

Thursday, April 7

12:00 noon

This same argument with myself has been going on since I finished writing on Monday, and maybe writing it will stop that and let it go on, go further in some way. I am going to take the rest of the term off. Two days of back and forth is enough. I will end the circular debate, the "should I/shouldn't I go to work" thing. Enough of that. Gather my strength and just move forward.

My little girl is really sad. She thinks she's been doing a bad job. That is not so, but she is still sad. I've been trying hard but right now I am just not okay. There is just something wrong with me, something I hope will get better, but right now I am just not okay.

Maybe tomorrow night I will work on the voice.

SESSION SEVEN

Saturday, April 9

Finding a target last night was hard. I read the journal from the week, and Nova seemed kind of upset about it. I knew I was being hard on myself. She asked if I really believed what I had written. Belief is a hard thing. I know things and I feel things and I believe things I both know and feel. When the two different processes coincide, then I believe.

We decided to target the wall in my mind. It is something I visualize, a wall that I push things behind. I feel like I have to use a lot of energy to keep things back there. It was a different kind of EMDR; we did not have a negative and positive cognition because I did not know what was there. The goal was just to think about the wall until it cracked, until I could see what was behind it. The clearest image of the wall comes from thoughts of work, so we used work.

I thought about work and the wall, about stuffing things behind the wall so I could go to work, watched Nova's fingers, and tried to see what was back there.

What came out was just a roar of **"YOU ARE A STUPID, STUPID GIRL! YOU ARE LAZY AND NO GOOD AND STUPID, STUPID, STUPID! I DON'T LIKE YOU, YOU STUPID GIRL, YOU! GO AWAY AND LEAVE ME ALONE. SHUT UP AND SIT DOWN, YOU STUPID GIRL!"**

The roar and the rage fill me right now, and it is still pretty strong but not as overwhelming. I almost panicked last night when the words came out in a loud voice that I did not recognize as mine. I felt lost for a moment, not able to control this voice. I wanted to get to most of the stuff we've done. I chose to go there and it was okay. Last night, for a space of time, it was just the roar and I couldn't stop it. I wanted to stop it. That was different; with the other things I have been very clear that I did not want to stop looking. I did not know that about the wall: I felt I had no choice.

I was amazed at the intensity of the ideas behind the wall, and also how young I was when I was hearing this. Nova prompts me to talk when she can see by my face that I am experiencing some emotions, and one of her prompts was about not being a [tenured] professor. For a split second I didn't know what it [a professor] was. Then I knew and was back to today and it was just funny. Didn't she know I wasn't in today, that the stupid stuff didn't come from today? The stupid stuff was from so long ago that my child who was talking then did not know what a professor was [much less what a tenured professor was]. It felt like seepage from behind the wall that affected me so much this week.

Who is saying that I am a stupid, stupid girl? Is it just me talking to myself? We talked about my parents last night. Was it them? I truly only remember one time that my mother told me I was doing something wrong, and that was hemming a skirt. She kept telling me to only use one thread, and I only had one thread on the needle. I could not understand what she was talking about; I just kept trying and my stitches got bigger and bigger as my eyes filled with tears until I could hardly see. I finally had to yell, "I only have one thread! What are you talking about?" So she explained that I should only catch one thread of the garment with my stitch, strong enough to hold but not pucker the fabric.

My father likes to tell a story about me. It has only occurred to me in the last few years how peculiar it is that he likes to tell it. I remember the start of the story. I know I am young because my head is about even with the door knob. I am going out the front door behind one of my brothers and he shuts the door on me. I think he hurt my foot. I get mad and call him a son of a bitch.

My dad is on the front porch and hears me. "Don't you say things about my wife!"

I remember being amazed that those words meant something about Mom. I only knew it was a bad thing to say to someone when you were mad at them.

The part that Dad tells is that he hit me on every step on the way upstairs. I guess he took me to my room. His story doesn't extend that far. He just says he hit me on every step, and he thinks this is a funny story. He laughs.

We covered such a range of things last night! I find that I am not sure when we were doing eye movements and when we weren't. I know that by the end of the night my eyes were really tired and kept trying to cross.

Nova and I talked about my envisioning alien things in my head. She said it wasn't really demons in me, though that was a Catholic way to look at it. That it was just parts of me.

I remember hollering at my son a lot, and hope he doesn't have me living in his head somewhere telling him he is stupid.

I have only covered a part of last night, but I am pretty tired so I am going to stop. The wall and the voice are not just about work; the stuff behind the wall doesn't know about work. Last night it seemed that the roar was all from back then, and I don't know who is saying [those things] to me.

Nova told me at the end of the session that last week was all pretty critical and mean to myself, and suggested that I re-read it and look at that.

NOVA'S COMMENTS ON SESSION SEVEN

When I met Mary for our seventh EMDR session, I was surprised and upset to find her depressed and angry with herself. She said, "It has taken me all this time to get to some really trite things, like that the people at work are individuals!" She seemed to have lost the blooming self-confidence she showed in early sessions, debating endlessly about whether or not she could, should, or would go to work. And then she talked about the wall behind which she stuffed bad things. It seemed the proper focus for the session. During EMDR, Mary looked and sounded like an angry child. She yelled, "You stupid, stupid, stupid! Sit down and shut up! You stupid girl!" Her tears were angry tears. After the session neither of us had an explanation for the anger or the insults. It didn't seem reasonable that it was little Mary talking. The wall had come down and left us totally bewildered.

INTERVAL SEVEN

Sunday, April 10

12:45 p.m.

I just reread part of yesterday, and there was something I didn't say that is pretty important. The stuff I have been going through about work and other things is very strange. That is clear to Nova, which is why she keeps focusing on work. I remember how I used to feel about work. For most of my jobs I remember waking up and being glad that I got to go to work, was anxious to get there and start enjoying myself. I am not sure when that changed, but the process now is very different.

I start several days beforehand, telling myself that I have to go to work. Then I start an internal process. What I usually do is let the dread start and then beat it back. This goes on for a long time. It has become almost unconscious, and now that I am becoming more aware of it I am not going to do that. The dread got stuffed behind the wall I talked about yesterday. It seems much clearer today what has been happening, and how the wall and the dread and the stuffing are all part of the same thing.

There is an incredible resistance inside me to many things. I am noticing it most in its absence, in that I feel no resistance at times now to going outside. There has been a lot of fighting going on inside me, so movement becomes difficult.

Part of the debate has been halted by turning the horror-filled events in my life into memories instead of reality. My fear has lessened so the part that says I have to hide, that I have to be careful, they can sense me, they will come ... that is quiet. That is just not true.

Another part is fed by the stuff I talked about yesterday. It is much more sophisticated and elusive when it seeps out from behind the wall than when I visualized the wall and tried to let stuff out. The stuff was very young in how it presented itself -- "YOU ARE

A STUPID, STUPID GIRL!" in that very loud voice. That is not going to convince me now. It may not have been anyone else but myself. Now I feel mostly just misplaced, not necessarily wrong or stupid.

I have almost two months off so I am going to keep looking and letting stuff out from behind the wall. This is a time for looking at all this resistance and watching and unlearning. I am not going to silence the negative murmurs, just try to hear them more clearly. What are they saying?

MONDAY, APRIL 11

9:45 a.m.

I go to a doctor tomorrow, and I find that I am nervous and scared. I am afraid that he will tell me that my seizures are all my fault. That is highly unlikely, but this discounting of myself, this fear that I am wrong, reminds me of my former boss. Nova and I talked about her yesterday. When I went to her with problems, she would turn it into a personal discussion of how sad it was that my life was so screwed up. She knew me from before I started having seizures; I worked there before I went to the UAE. Anyway, she built on my feelings of inadequacies every time I talked to her, and I collapsed under that. She really was pretty nasty to me, and I stuffed all my anger. Dealing with my new boss is a totally different experience, but I may need some more defusing from the experience with my former boss to make work an okay place to be.

Meanwhile, I am having a good day. Today, I'm just going to enjoy the day. It is beautiful, and there are lots of new things coming up in my yard that I need to uncover. Tomorrow is garbage day, and I still get a thrill from having the city take away bags and bags of the leaves and branches for free. I had to pay extra in Ohio. It's nice to enjoy the simple things in life

SESSION EIGHT

Friday, April 15

We didn't do any EMDR last night. What we did was talk about many things.

The wall is in ruins. It is incredible to me, but I can see myself wandering around, looking in the corners with a little flashlight, and there is nothing there. How amazing! There was nothing there but the loud voice saying, "You stupid, stupid girl!"

Nova talked about how emotions come first and then thoughts. The emotional content was the "You are a stupid girl!" stuff, which does not hurt. The me repeating that voice is definitely a kid. Once I knew it was a young me repeating things, it lost its power.

Things seem so much clearer to me. I have blocked the knowledge that some of the men at the club [where I go to meetings] are interested in me. I noticed it finally, and I have to say they do not interest me!

I want to spend time with very few people in Lansing. There are many things I find interesting, but my interests aren't shared by a lot of people. That doesn't mean anyone is wrong or right; it just means we are different, and I don't want to pretend that I am not.

Nova asked why I am not rich and famous. I must admit I wonder that as well! At 21, I was running a social welfare program with a staff of about 20 or so, dealing with 150 kids. Writing proposals, getting money, having a good time. Then the drinking started, and it was downhill for a while. Then [I] dropped off the edge, with the banner year of horror. Got sober, got involved with Bill, the man I married. I know I felt safe with him. We were essential to each other during that second year of sobriety, when my mother and brother died, and his mother and father died. It was a hard year for both of us, and we made it through sober. We tried to make it more than that, but we had little in common. And to save that marriage, I left grad school in physics, which was fascinating.

Incredibly difficult, requiring a lot of work, but fascinating. It [leaving grad school] did not save the marriage.

I do not believe that I am a stupid girl. But I still don't know where that came from.

NOVA'S COMMENTS ON SESSION EIGHT

Rereading this section several months later, Mary said, "I can't remember this part. It sounds as if I'm trying to make everything okay. I think I was whistling in the dark!" In this session, I was just relieved that she seemed to have regained her self-confidence, that the treatment was still working and helping her to a different place. Definitely the treatment was still working, but Mary was headed for some strange and unexpected places. It wasn't time yet for the happy ending.

INTERVAL EIGHT

Saturday, April 16

7:00 a.m.

I am feeling pretty good about myself today. As I look back, my life has been pretty interesting most of the time. Helping establish a basic math program for the UAE University was not the only time I was challenged and did worthwhile things. The work I was doing before I left for the UAE verged on the all-consuming, which seems to be the kind of work I like. While I was working at the community college, I was also the coordinator of a statewide organization, the Up and Out of Poverty Campaign, dealing with welfare reform [coming out of my work with Michigan Welfare Rights] I should get out the scrapbooks of that time, and see how many years I got to follow at every stage the legislation as it went through the state legislature. I am pulled to politics, have been since first grade. That was pretty wild. I wrote proposals to get the money for the campaign because I had been doing essentially the same work for free, but had lost health benefits and needed them. So I got them by getting myself paid for what I wanted to do.

I am a pretty competent person!

I need to decide what to do with my life, and it seems there are many things to look at. Part of the reason I loved being overseas was the safety issue. Now that I am safe in this country, the world can open back up.

I am going to re-read all of this stuff and put it all in my new perspective. How very quickly this is all happening! I am light-years from where I was just a little while ago.

5:15 p.m.

It has been such a wonderful day. I don't even know why; it just seems like I am so much better than I have been. I am hopeful that I will get better, that I can pick another thing to do with my life. I am listening to music and thinking about making some instead of just singing along. My guitar is still with me.

I've been playing my game online, and went to the library and the pharmacy and to the ATM machine and to the hardware store. My goodness! I did some yoga and did dishes and I am still full of energy! Will continue cleaning the winter debris from the back yard right after I put up a hook for my robe in my bedroom. WOW! This is like a week's worth of stuff for me!

Neurons firing in a good way today. Think I'll just enjoy and start digging tomorrow.

Sunday, April 17

7:45 a.m.

I am luxuriating in the feeling that there are many things that it would be fun to do. It seems so strange to realize that this feeling did not used to come very often. I feel alive again. The world is to play in.

I will do some work today because I want to! What a rush! I wish there were three of me so I could do everything! Instead of attempting to find one in a long list of things that doesn't seem too overwhelming, I want to do them all! I have a backlog of things I want to write, and one already written for the Garden Project newsletter, part of my continuing series called "Hints from the Clueless." There really is a place in teaching for those who have to concentrate on the basics, things that to others are obvious.

Play some music. Continue working on decluttering my house. My bedroom is so austere I just love it! Yoga. Write Bob. A walk would be nice, to check out all the things growing in the neighborhood. Finish a few dishes so my kitchen sparkles. Lots of the usual things, but they all sound good. It is pretty scary to look at that change.

I'm remembering when I was in therapy in Ohio for a while, and one of the things the therapist concentrated on with me was why I felt that I had to take care of myself as a child. Boy, did she have the wrong take on it! Anyway, I found myself one day, in my mind, back in the crib, screaming and crying and no one came. Part of me was watching that, but alas, the one in charge of my mouth was the baby. And the baby was screaming.

She told me that I had to stop, that it was time to go, but I couldn't. She called the ambulance on me. They were all pretty mean to me, both the paramedics and the doctor once I got to the hospital. They just kept telling me to stop. I did after they gave me a lot of drugs. For a seemingly long time, I was very afraid that I would spontaneously become that screaming child again. So was the therapist. We were not a good match.

I know that I have changed. I have been aware of that as I have gone through life. But the putting it together, the "how do I go from one way to another way,"... that is a hard thing. I've thought about writing the story of my life, and that is the thing I noticed. Bob called it a "sense of continuity of self." I certainly lost that feeling for a while. It was more like a series of disconnected events and situations, and me sitting there saying, "How did this happen? Who am I?"

It's time for my meeting, so I have to stop.

7:40 p.m.

Feeling connected and alive, loved and useful and accepted, and thinking about my safe place, leading the children in song for the Children's Mass in the UAE. What an incredible rush that was. There was nothing the least bit wrong about it; it was just totally right and totally wonderful. That sense of community and total usefulness and support is what I think draws me back to the Catholic Church. I'm looking for that. But I didn't go to Mass this weekend, so that means it's not the Church's teachings but something else.

After all these years I am still searching for my relationship to the problems in the world, and what my part of a solution can be. That also seems wrong in some way.

The wall is down, but the seepage affected a lot of me. That is how I'm thinking as I notice the continuing changes in me. Some are subtle; some are really obvious. But it is a matter of noticing them first. I may try to just think of lots of things and see which things cause conflict when I think of them. I can use that as a basis of the EMDR stuff. Nothing that I can think is off limits. And so I will have to look at many things, to see what I really believe.

For Thursday: The church. The problems of the world. Assuming all the responsibility for relationships. Let's see how many other things there are that that give me a gut feeling that my thinking and feeling about them are screwed up.

10:00 p.m.

Add another to that list of things; add the line that no one is going to help me, that I am alone. That may be what I am trying prevent with Bob. That is the fear; that is the pull. What the hell am I doing with him? I think it is some more stuff from behind the wall. I thought it was empty, but I just caught a wayward thought about how Bob will keep me from being alone. But it's seepage, I think. Seepage from what I thought was the ruins.

I sound like I am crazy. But I am not. There is stuff left that we need to work on, that I can and will face, but it is not happening tonight. I am too scared. I do not want the little girl to come out and cry and scream. Please. I will let the little girl scream if that is what she wants/needs when Nova is here and I will be okay, and I will have the safe place if I need it. I will be okay, and I will not forget it, because I have it written down here. I can just relax tonight. If there is something else I have to write, I will. But it is down and I don't have to think about it now. It will be okay. The time will come to face it, but I at least don't have to face it alone. I will be okay. Calm down here: you will be okay, little one. It is okay.

I am angry that [the doctors and psychiatrists and therapists] did not know about EMDR therapy, that no one is standing on roof tops hollering about it. They are too busy pushing drugs.

I am scared. I wish Nova was here. My little girl is upset. I am upset. I don't want to scream. I want some food, some chocolate. I thought the food thing was gone, but it helps push down this stuff. I don't want to think about it right now. Not right now. It is not a good time.

Monday, April 18

11:30 a.m.

As I reread the stuff from last night, I know it is that voice again, or maybe there are [multiple] voices. They aren't loud when I hear them. They are whispers I catch in the corner of my mind and try to grab before they run away. It's probably not a good time to go searching for them when it is late and I am tired. If I hadn't been successful at being firm with myself about looking at it later, I would have called Nova and asked for help. It was hard to keep my little girl calm, and hard to not listen to the voices.

I haven't had many physical things [coming out of EMDR], just the ones about being taller, about my body becoming my body rather than the armor that I lived in, the idea that my house was bigger and it was mine. I'm having a new one. I've been missing the ring that Dennis gave me. Dennis is the man I was with for almost six of the 11 years I was sickest. I met him online, and he moved in with me a short while after I first met him face-to-face. He was the first person I met who could stop a seizure with the touch of his hand.

Anyway, I stopped wearing the ring I got from Dennis a while ago, both because it was tight and because I didn't want to think about him. My hand is now feeling too light; I will be doing something else and find myself checking the finger I wore the ring on, looking for it.

I have been downplaying the whole thing with Dennis. It fell apart when I went through menopause and so enjoyed not being driven by my libido that I didn't want to have sex at all. He had decided he wanted to become a game developer/computer programmer. He was much younger than me. I took his thought and helped make it a reality. But none of his family had ever been to college; most of them had never finished high school. He didn't know what he was getting into, and freaked out, and I just kept pushing him along.

So he ran online and found someone. And moved the minute I asked what he was doing playing online with some girl when he was supposed to be going to classes, supposed to be talking to me.

Not a good situation. But I'd said our entire time together that he would have to leave me and go find some young girl and have babies. That was supposed to protect me from falling in love and getting hurt. He keeps in touch, and is working on having a family. I think it's time I admit that I got hurt and move on from there.

Is this moving forward or backwards? I don't know.

Tuesday, April 19

10:00 a.m.

I certainly feel high today! Smiling and laughing and giggling. What a wonderful day yesterday was! How nice today is going to be!

It was good all day long. It is so nice to have full days of doing things that I want to do. I can tell how much I have changed, and I'm still just loving it.

Rob called yesterday, my friend from the UAE. It was good to hear his voice. He is an amazing person. I remember the first time I was aware of being by myself and not thinking at all. Not as part of an activity designed to get me there, like meditation, but as a thing which happened on its own. I was sitting in the back yard and just being aware of the yard. I think Rob spends a lot of time in this place, being attuned to the present. Anyway, we talked about the EMDR stuff. He asked, "What made you give vitality to those memories?" I had a quick spurt of understanding, followed by a blanking of my mind to what he had said. I asked him to repeat it so I could write it down.

And I just heard from Bob. He's going to be in Michigan, and will be coming here for a while. I am filled with joy and excitement and anticipation. I expect to spend a lot of time laughing and playing. I think this will be great.

Enough of the diary stuff.

I have to know that this joy and release are a beginning and not an end. I do not want to think of that. I want to think that I am done and the whole thing will be solved. Like I got my arteries artificially scraped so my blood flows better, which makes me think better and move easier and all kinds of great things. But under the problem of clogged arteries are all kinds of things that contributed to their being clogged, and if I am not careful and watchful, that process will start again. The stuffing is habitual now and it would be easy to start again. Maybe I did not notice the problem starting. How could I not have noticed?

I am noticing that I have been using a lot of sentence fragments and many qualifiers, and am consciously trying not do that. Finish the thought, state the fact. The qualifiers are a hedge to what I say. "It seems," "It is like" -- those back me away from looking long enough to say "it is," to think whether it is or is not my reality. "It's just" is a diminishing thing. When I use that word "just," I am telling myself that it is not important.

Moving on to topics/statements that strike a chord in me. The problems of the world. I would like to know why I feel so guilty, so responsible. I did something wrong so the world is screwed up. Is it that I feel I am so powerful that my attention/non-attention to a problem makes so much difference? Is it that I think I am god? Or is it being a part of a group that is important? Is it that in the church I had a part to play as a member of the group and the group as a whole was working on all the problems? I don't think I could have worked in Welfare Rights if I didn't know that others were working in the same way, from the same shared understanding, in the peace movement, in the housing arena, in health care and education.

My "things to write" file is full of newspaper articles that in my opinion need a response. I decide which of the many to actually engage [in] based on the insistence of the response that keeps composing itself in my head. I write those things I cannot avoid writing.

I have to do a lot more thinking and watching on this one before I can get to the simple statements that are required for the EMDR procedure to begin. The list of ideas runs from my mind just like the list of the three traumas did. I have a hard time holding them there. At least I got them down before they ran away.

3:45 p.m.

Why am I so sad right now? What's wrong? It is all the things that I think are wrong, that should be changed, and there isn't enough time in my life to fight all of them.

This is the overwhelming idea that I was trying to think about this morning, that "the world is so incredibly wrong in a basic way" idea that is so large and yet in reality is circular in all its manifestations.

I was remembering this earlier, but today I am feeling it. I feel it in wanting to cry. I feel a tenseness in my throat. I want to scream, "I'm mad as hell and I'm not going to take it anymore!" My day is an endless series of small defenses of self. I feel it in the pit of my stomach, and it makes me want to throw up. Playing the national anthem brings on some of the feeling; I always cry when I hear it, except for the Jimi Hendrix version on the Woodstock album.

I just talked to Phyllis and the mood lifted. Just zeroing in on the issue for Thursday will be enough for now. Looking at the instruction sheet Nova left, I need:

presenting issue or memory: being immobilized by the changes going on in this country

picture: being eaten alive by businesses and government agencies, surrounded by all these folks taking little bites out of me

the negative cognition: they are too much for me, they will bring me down

the positive cognition:

The positive cognition will be hardest to figure out. I'd like to see positive in everything! But that would mean that I'd get to remake the world, and I don't think I can do that.

Nova said last week that the simplest explanation is the correct one, the Occam's razor principle that is used in science as well. She was talking about the way I am so down on myself for not noticing the obvious, the simple things, in my reactions to people. Simple does not necessarily mean black and white though. I was headed there, but that is wrong. I do not need to come out with a simple explanation of how the world works.

Maybe I would like to believe that I am part of the world and not in charge of it.

There is a part of the negative belief and picture that has to do with [the belief that] I should be able to fight them. I should be able to change it, that idea of responsibility.

I learned in the fourth step [of my 12-step program] when I did an inventory of my life, that the facts of the situation do not and never did cause me to do or feel something. My reaction is my purview. The fact that the Vietnam War went on too long was not a reason for me to feel personally guilty. Looking at that now, it does appear much simpler!

These ramblings may get me to see more of what is going on.

I've been thinking that the spiritual connection between people and the rest of creation may be the key point.

The positive for this is hard to see. It was hard to figure for the other things as well. For them it was because I believed that the evil could sense me and come after me, that it was impossible to think that I wasn't a target. Just stating what I believe now (that there is evil, that it may find me, but only when I am so drunk and reckless that I ignore what I know and have no common sense) was a leap of faith. It may be that I will find a view that I will like.

That may just be bullshit, though. I didn't imagine that the biggest thing that I missed in the whole "crazy man-hostage" thing was that I was overjoyed when he raped me. Or that the sight of the kids with their footed pajamas in the neighbor's house would make me realize what the neighbor's viewpoint was. Those things came out of the EMDR, out of the reprocessing. I didn't know them and could not have predicted them before. Maybe we will just go with the image of the negative and see what happens.

Wednesday, April 20

4:00 p.m.

It may be that the problem is not solving how I can impact the world. It may be the problem is the belief that it *should* be fair. My outrage isn't based on the belief that it should be different, but that I am responsible in some way. It was no problem in the UAE; I did not feel guilty that it wasn't fair. I did everything I could to make it better for those who were having trouble. That may be the positive, that it is not my fault in any way that things are wrong.

SESSION NINE

Friday, April 22

It wasn't until I was rereading the journal prior to the session and trying to figure out what we were going to do that I noticed that, except for two short incidents, my whole week was great! It was hard work some days and on some topics, but almost all of the week was full of wonderful things, and I was sorry that the days were not longer. It used to be that the only time I was sure that I would be content was when I settled down in bed for some rest. There was nothing I had to try to get myself to do then but rest. What a difference now!

Before Nova got here, I spent about an hour trying to get something together in the form that the EMDR folks recommend. I ended up with this

Presenting issue: My reaction to the changes and problems in the U.S.

Picture: myself getting eaten alive by the government and businesses in this country.

Negative cognition: There is something I should be doing about it, but it is too overwhelming. I can't understand how it happened, and that's a personal failure

Positive cognition: I had some wimpy thing, like *"I will learn to break it down and feel that I can manage to live in the face of it all."*

I had a list of changes and recent U.S. policies that cause me to be angry and make me want to scream. I figured that looking at all of them at once would kick me into something. I think I could have written for an hour, but I stopped after Nova got here.

Things started falling into place. I started really hearing them when I read them to Nova. As I read about how I handled the loss of my insurance, it hit me how remarkable that was. When I lost my health insurance, I developed a proposal and got funding for the Up and Out of Poverty Campaign, based on a Massachusetts model. It continued what I was doing on the legislative end [with

Michigan Welfare Rights] but added some travel around the state talking to groups, doing workshops, and in general really broadening the group involved in legislative action from the recipient groups to agencies, unions, and churches. The grant covered my travel expenses and paid enough to buy into a health insurance program at the church that agreed to administer the grant.

It hit me that this was an unusual thing to do, that most people would not have done that. Most people would not have thought of it, and even if they did, would not have been able to pull it off. How incredible it was that I did that! How lame my comment when I first wrote it : "I am a competent person." Competent, hell! I can do amazing things!

We spent some time talking about the statement, "Now that I am safe in this country, the world can open back up." I feel like I have just graduated from college and my whole life lies ahead of me!

I read faster and faster after that, whipping through things and expanding on them with new feelings and intensity. We talked about the woman who was my counselor in Hamilton. She did not believe that I was capable of much. Community mental health programs can be deadly. They often set the bar really low, and discount things that don't fit into their worldview. A friend of mine was caught in the system. He came from a background of wealth, now gone, and that affected him a lot. They thought that was a delusion. It's hard to get better when therapists don't believe you! For my part, I managed to get a new health plan and then a new therapist.

Nova does not assume things about the people she works with. She is incredible. She is willing to follow my lead, willing to see things from my perspective, willing to let me be myself and define my own life. I know we have a special relationship because we have been good friends for at least 24 years. She had seen me do things that do not fit into my current image of myself at all.

As we talked it burst into my mind that I did not need to subject myself to some group discipline and limits in order to work. I might join some groups once I figure out what I want to do. I will find people to work with; I will come to know and support in some way the people who are working on the issues I don't work on. But I can be me, as challenged and innovative and combative and clear as I possibly can,

Every page of last week's journal held something that I didn't truly get until I read some of it and talked to her about it.

The two upsetting times that I wrote about were no longer upsetting when I read them. It did not seem real that they had upset me so much at the time.

The section where I talked about being angry that EMDR isn't more readily available just became a discussion with Nova that I approach Oprah Winfrey about the issue. Nova thinks I would be great. I didn't convince her that she would be great, but I will next time. Oprah can get Francine Shapiro, the woman who discovered the technique by accident and who has copyrighted it. There is absolutely no reason in the world not to go for it. I'm not finished. I may never be finished with this discovery process, but what I have learned and done so far is incredible.

My sexual desire has come back. That was something that I hadn't mentioned in the journal. But it's been inching its way into my life through awareness of the people around me, through some of the online and email play I have been doing. Then came the whole physical thing of missing Dennis's ring. Reading it again, it made so much more sense. I really was hurt in that relationship. I had convinced myself that since I went into it knowing and saying that it was limited in time, it would not hurt when he left. I was just wrong! My intellect does not control my emotions. I look at it now as something I could have avoided. But I can just know better the next time. It's not that I cannot allow there to be a next time. It's not that I can never fall in love again. One of the first things I learned in recovery was that I didn't have to sleep with everyone who wanted to sleep with me. I did not have to justify being selective; I could just say no. Now I'm learning that just because I feel something I don't have to pursue it if I know that it won't work, that it isn't a good match, that I'm not being some kind of snob. I'm just being me. I don't have to get into unequal, doomed relationships. Duh!

We changed the positive statement to "I can change the world." I have changed the world in little ways. I think of Mothers Against Drunk Driving and all that they accomplished, and all the parents who have pushed for changes in the treatment of missing children. I think of the changes in dealing with domestic assault — not perfect, but a long way from where it used to be. An old friend of mine is now the national coordinator for the Families Against Mandatory Minimums. As a result of her work, that law has been repealed in several states. About a month ago I ran into her but have not followed up on her invitation to get together and talk because I felt incapable of operating on that level. If I don't find her card, I will find her website! I'm ready to go for it!

We did not do any eye movements last night. We ended the session because my eyes felt tired. As I read through Tuesday in particular, some of the words and sentences made no sense to me. As I look at it now, I can see that I wrote some things I disagree with. I think that the reading, the back and forth, very fast reading and crossing out, was enough of the side-to-side stimulation that it worked. I've had six other sessions, so I know that particular tiredness that I get as a result of EMDR, and that is what I felt.

NOVA'S COMMENTS ON SESSION NINE

Both Mary and I had a difficult time with this interval and session. "What's all this about"? Mary takes off on politics and social justice. Why? Until now, the writing and the sessions have dealt with personal experiences and their reevaluation. The change is probably explained when she says, "I want to think I am done and the 'whole thing' is solved." She doesn't really want to look further. But she is on a journey that's not easy to cancel. She says, "I would like to know why I feel so guilty, so responsible. I did something wrong and so the whole world is wrong." Her journey isn't over, no matter how she puts up walls of words to avoid it. And her intuition seems to be telling her that the hardest part is still to come. Who wouldn't want to grab the good stuff, and get out before everything falls apart??

INTERVAL NINE

Wednesday, April 27

11:20 a.m.

It has been five days since I wrote anything. I feel like I have been on vacation. Bob was here last weekend and I had a wonderful time. It was just us in our own space. I couldn't believe how comfortable I was with him, how much we connected with each other. There was no doubt that we cared about each other and had been important in each other's lives. The time seemed too short.

I was totally shocked at how I felt when he left. I really missed him, which made no sense to me. I wanted to make up a story line for what we were doing, but resisted that. Why was I so sad? I finally just went with being sad because he wasn't there.

Today was an eighth-step meeting, making a list of all persons we had harmed. I thought about Bob and how I insisted that he allow me the room to sleep with other people while simultaneously being my own true love. I was so very selfish. But in order to compromise, to change your behavior consciously to meet someone else's needs, you have to be pretty sure of who you are and what is important to you.

Today I want to think about the next session, which will be tomorrow or Friday. I'm thinking about my body size.

There are two basic things involved here, or at least two things I have noticed. One is food itself as a quick fix. The other is the bonus I get from being overweight. I want to look at the second one first.

I have talked about my weight keeping me safe, disguising me from predators. It has also made me feel insulated from the people around me. A striking example is after the divorce when Bill moved in next door to me. I gained 20 pounds in a month. It put distance between Bill and me. My weight also gives me an image of myself that I am less than other people. I can't be rich and famous if I am so fat. I can't get into a relationship with a person who is an achiever and stable and growing if I am fat. It is part of my self-definition as a broken person.

People do look at you differently when you are really overweight. They discount what you say, think of you as being less intelligent. I really can't get all excited about that being a bad thing, because it is a choice that I make about how I present myself to the world. My weight has gone up and down a lot. If I am feeling safe, it is okay to lose weight. It is a self-imposed difference, and I've never been able to see the prejudice against fat people as a real issue to fight about. It is a convenient excuse to justify your lack of progress in the world. I am this way because it is useful to me in some way to be this way.

When I was in the UAE, I lost a lot of weight. It was a byproduct of being happy, I think, and feeling good about myself. When I got back to this country, I immediately started gaining weight. It was the safety issue. As I battled it I would say to myself that it was okay, that men didn't get too excited and insistent until I hit a certain weight, that it was okay for a while. I became more conscious of the part of me that so wanted to walk and run and hike, but couldn't. The voice that would say, "Do we get to stop eating yet? Can we stop eating?"

I lost some weight last year, my goal being to be able to dance all night at Jon's wedding. I thought in terms of the steady decrease in weight I had experienced before, looked at the clothes I had in terms of how to prepare for changing a clothing size every month or so, and how to build a wardrobe for that situation. Then all hell broke loose in Jon's marriage and I ran to food.

Thinking in terms of EMDR and looking back at what I did earlier, I would like to look at my reactions to two scenarios: that point when I feel the weight just flowing off me and when I examine my reactions visualizing myself at a normal weight. I'll have to look at the issue definition sheet and work that out.

In addition, there is the idea of food as an instant way to change the way I feel. If I can't sleep I can eat a lot of carbs and I will be able to sleep. If I am feeling sad, sugar in the form of ice cream or cake or cookies can give me an instant high. This is like the alcoholic thing. Like alcohol, I will probably have to detox and learn to deal with my emotions in different ways. I may want to think of a scenario to use the EMDR with this issue.

This coming session is the last one we have scheduled.

11:00 p.m.

I don't think I am good enough. What is that about? It can't just be weight; it doesn't feel like just weight. What is it that I think is so wrong with me? I've been in a bad mood and teary most of today. What do I think is so wrong with me?

Thursday, April 28

6:15 a.m.

I had no self-doubt last weekend with Bob. I didn't worry about what I should or shouldn't say or do, or that I had no right to be with him. Maybe that is what is hitting me hard.

I have been thinking for so long that he was part of another life, of the life when I wasn't defective in some basic way. He was the last man I was with that was a match for me, my equal in intelligence and understanding. He came from the group of men that would have been considered normal and natural for me.

I have to wonder if there was something in our relationship that changed me, or if it was the drugs and alcohol. There is a hard-core belief in me, that I can't see the start of, that says I am not worthy of that kind of man. This is very strange. A deep sadness wells up in me, and I don't know where it comes from. What is wrong? Why shouldn't I be with Bob or someone like Bob? Why is he too good for me?

Am I a bad girl? Am I a mean girl? What is so wrong with me? I am broken. I just broke. It was just too much and I broke. Life broke me, and I'm not going to be fixed. I can't do what other people do.

What do they do?

They cut themselves off from all the bad things, they don't know the bad things, they pretend that they are whole.

Or are we back to the stupid stuff? Is that still there?

I should have known ...

What? What should I have known? What did I forget this weekend that I usually know, all the time, at some level? I didn't know it this weekend. It was so very easy to be with him. What did I forget?

I felt like I was a normal person, important to him. He is important to me. Why is it stupid for me to think that I am important to him?

A trip to another reality, and then a crashing back to where I am now. I am trying to figure out what the crash was about.

It started with him leaving. Do I think they will always leave? Is it about being left? I always expect to be left. I know it is coming, that it will end. Is that it? No.

Is it peculiar to him? Is it about him, about Bob? The merge I felt when I first met him, the delight, the amazing specialness that was us? I can't forget the joy that was meeting him. The freedom to be all of me. And that was what it was this weekend. We were safe together: we could talk about anything and I was safe and understood and accepted. If I imagine our hands touching, it seems that life is the way it should be. What is this about?

He is himself, he is special, and we become a "we" so easily.

I don't know if it is him or some big group that he represents.

Let me remember. I wasn't devastated when we broke up so long ago. I was bewildered. I didn't believe it could happen. I was lost. Some part of me that I took for granted wasn't there all of a sudden.

When he left after last weekend and it sank in that he was gone, it was like my heart being ripped out. In the space we created together, there was no evil, no pain, just joy in being myself and in Bob being himself. I felt complete and full. It was a time of heightened awareness on one level and a time of forgetting of self.

10:00 a.m.

Well, tonight is the next session. I have to get ready for it.

It hit me in the meeting that when I am on the phone with Bob I feel broken. It feels like I am pretending to be okay and I am not, and that he doesn't really know who he is talking to. That isn't true in person and it isn't true online. But the feeling is definitely like I am broken.

So, how am I broken?

It might be easier to look at when I broke. I broke when I got back to the States from the UAE. At first I was just freaking out inside at the kind of life that was here, believing that the world had gone crazy. It really was the world that horrified me in the book *1984*. Lots of those changes had to do and continue to have to do with technology, with the computer and information age.

I do not want to keep up with the changes, and there is part of me that thinks I cannot keep up with the changes.

Cell phones seem very strange things. People talk about different plans and combinations of plans and costs per minute and I am back at "Why in the world is anyone even interested in this?" That world has passed me by.

It's like a big piece of life that everyone gets but me. If that is my reality and the limits of it as well, why am I not okay with it? Is it that I feel so unable to bridge the gap, to even see the point of view of those who think differently from me? That some fact is so self-evident to me that I cannot understand how it is not self-evident to others?

I know there are other things in the mix when it comes to the pivotal point, the return from the UAE. The safety thing I've talked about and hopefully put to rest. The societal changes that were a weird form of culture shock that I never got over. Is there a spiritual part as well? The sense of disconnection that I feel from the community around me. It may be the same thing as culture shock, but just a different aspect of it.

This issue is for another time. I want to do the weight thing tonight, and need to get that into shape. I want to look at the bonuses I get from being overweight.

SESSION TEN

Friday, April 29

Last night I read Nova everything I had written. The feeling of the world being open to me, of me being a dancing star came back. Then the interlude, the vacation with Bob. Nova saw the grief at his leaving as a natural reaction to a sparkling time.

The whole weight thing has been an issue for a while, and I picked it not because it was growing out of something current but because it was "on my plate." It was something that needed to be done before we were finished. As I read, it seemed much of it was already finished. I no longer fear predators lying in wait for me, so I don't need the disguise of carrying a lot of weight. I feel perfectly capable of saying no to men that I am not interested in, just because I am not interested in them! That feels very good, and I know it is true as I think about some of the men in my life at this moment. I have no problem with losing weight. I will be okay. That came as we talked while I was reading.

Nova and I looked at what I had written about the weight issue. I have gotten very scared in the past when I felt the weight just melting off, but that isn't true anymore. It was the second image I talked about that resonated. I am thin and active. How do I feel?

I don't deserve to be thinner and alive. I don't deserve to sparkle. The weight keeps me from some things that I want but I can't have them. Why? Because I was broken.

That was what I didn't feel this weekend. I didn't feel broken. It wasn't self-doubt that was missing; it was the whole idea that I didn't deserve to be okay because I was broken and couldn't be fixed. That had no part of the weekend with Bob, and that was what was still left with the weight issue as well.

Start of Session

Negative Cognition: I am broken and useless. Belief: highest on the scale
Positive Cognition: I am not broken, I am strong. Belief: lowest on the scale

We tried a series of eye movements involving the phone and not answering it because I was broken, since I had a clear feeling from that. It didn't work. I looked back in the journal for the place where my voice had gotten high, my little girl's voice, and my eyes had teared up. I found it yesterday morning early. *"Am I a bad girl? Am I a mean girl? What is so wrong with me? I am broken. I just broke. It was just too much and I broke. Life broke me and I am not going to be fixed."* That was the feeling.

Nova helped me look for the time when I was not broken, for the actual time that I broke. I was not broken in the UAE. I was not broken when I first got back. I came back to Michigan first, where Tommy Walker's sister, Beth's [other] Aunt Mary, was dying. I wasn't broken through that. I got to Arizona not broken.

I broke when I was teaching chemistry at the all-girls Catholic high school in Phoenix. I hated that job. I hated the way I was treated. I hate chemistry! Everything that I knew about teaching I wasn't allowed to do. Why didn't I quit?

I got the job in February. Jon and I had settled in Tempe in late August. I picked Arizona because I so love the desert. I picked Tempe for Jon, because I had come back for his education and Tempe had the best schools I could find in Arizona. I started a job search, and looked at going to Arizona State to get a master's in math. I was open to possibilities.

I was looking for the hand of God in my life. I had been used to that, and while the idea of God has been pretty broad throughout my sobriety, in the UAE God became Catholic for me. I worked some Manpower temp jobs while other things were going in process. At the same time I got an adjunct teaching job at a junior college at one of the malls.

I was thinking in terms of substitute teaching when I applied to the Phoenix Catholic schools, but the high school had just lost a chemistry teacher several weeks into the second semester. So I entered the world of high school teaching.

That was what I thought of as Nova and I started the eye movements again, being at the school, in front of the class, breaking. As I watched her fingers, the anger came out, the rage at how I was treated, at what I was expected to do. At how dreadful it was, how much I did not want to be there. There was nothing about the job I enjoyed.

But I had said I would do it. I was stuck.

I was also terrified. All the fear about predators came back, fierce after its absence in the UAE. People were murdered daily in the Phoenix area. Carrying concealed weapons was legal. Ads on the radio offered to teach women how to shoot to protect themselves.

And I broke. I fell apart. It was just too much.

But I didn't think of quitting, didn't think of getting another job. It was the Catholics.

End of Session

Negative Cognition: I am broken and useless. Belief: almost lowest on the scale

Positive Cognition: I am not broken, I am strong. Belief: almost highest on the scale

As Nova and I talked after the EMDR, I remembered the call from a professor who was interested in talking to me about working with him. He was interested because of the work that I had been doing in the UAE. I didn't even think of the possibility of quitting and doing that.

I have to work some on saying no to people, on looking out for myself and not always looking out for someone or something else.

The fact is I was expecting too much of myself. I am not there. I am not broken now. I am okay.

NOVA'S COMMENTS ON SESSION TEN

Between sessions nine and ten Mary had a visit from the man with whom, 35 years ago, she had her idealized "Perfect Love Relationship." They seemed to have an idyllic meeting, needing no other people, talking for hours, playing music they both loved, taking walks where she introduced him to her favorite trees and flowers. When he left it was not surprising to me that Mary was sad, but she was very surprised at how devastated she felt. She didn't expect to cry and feel so bereft. She realized she had the thought, "I'm not good enough for him .... There is a hard-core belief in me

.... that says I am not worthy of that kind of man. This is very strange." She started to wonder why she felt that way. What was so wrong with her? She said in her "little girl" voice, "*Am I a bad girl? Am I a mean girl? What is so wrong with me?*" And then she got an answer that felt true. "*I am broken.*" In the tenth session Mary found out again how much of her freedom of choice was controlled by the beliefs of her "little girl."

INTERVAL TEN

Friday, April 29

7:30 a.m.

I want to sing and dance, have actually done some dancing, even though it is morning and you can see directly into my house from the street or the neighbors'! I want to run and swim and turn cartwheels. I am not broken.

3:00 p.m.

I am still feeling pretty good. Now that I have settled into my body, it is feeling smaller today. I just got up from my nap, and dreamed about jogging.

It is strange to think in terms of taking care of myself. I am still a little uncomfortable with that idea! Taking care of others, that is good. Saying no when someone asks me to do something for them will be harder. I have just gotten where I don't feel I have to explain my physical limitations, that I can just say no. The next step is to say no because I don't want to.

It makes me nervous to think about what I am going to do with my life now. It's scary. What I really want to do right now is work on my body. Enjoy the summer. Walk. Garden. Do yoga. Find a place to swim. Find someone to dance with and a place to dance. Just get in shape. The world is looking pretty big at the moment. I don't want to tackle it all at once, just a little bit at a time.

I went to my [12-step] meeting and then stopped by to see someone in the hospital, then went to physical therapy. All in a row! I parked far away so I got to walk some and felt strong and healthy when I walked.

Jon called and asked if I'd run off a copy of the event center schedule for MSU from online. He will come here to get it and I can give him his mail then. I will not take it there to him. They have a car. It took me a long time to say no to my son, but I got there.

I also told Jon I wouldn't pick him up at work at 2 a.m. on a regular basis because it was the middle of the night and way too far to drive. I said I wasn't doing well lately and wasn't even working right now. I had to justify it. Having seizures is a good excuse and lets me take care of myself. It forces me to take care of myself. If it's just me giving and no one willing to help me in return, it's not okay.

8:30 p.m.

I wrote to Bob not long ago and noticed something strange. My attitude towards websites and computers in general has changed. I wonder if it will affect other things.

I also felt more flexible and confident walking today. I found myself shutting the front door and noticed that I hadn't reattached the drainpipe when I mowed the grass. I just went out and did it, no impact on my body at all. Very cool, just like a normal person, like an unbroken person.

Interesting stuff!!

Saturday, April 30

7:45 a.m.

Just spent the last hour and a half writing Bob and dancing. Most of yesterday's journal was work, looking at the idea of taking care of myself, saying no. Right now, I'm in the discovery mode, which is so much easier!

So many good things to do. Oh, yes, I like this.

I want to think through the idea of tough love. I've thought in the past that it was overused, that it was a way to disconnect from another person. It seems to me today, looking at my relationship with my son, that it is not a disconnect.

Living through his suicide attempt and returning to his wife, knowing that he is treated poorly, I was frantic to find something I could do to change his life for him, to help him find his way out.

The reality is he doesn't want out right now, and I still do not know that he won't prove to be a source of change for her.

Anything can happen in this world, however unlikely it may seem to me.

I am recognizing that I cannot do anything but love him. I can let him know I love him, that I am here, that I will be here regardless of anything. That doesn't mean I have to give him my money and my time and all the space in my head. I don't have to go down with him.

It was hard for me to get there. And that is part of taking care of myself.

Sunday, May 1

10:00 a.m.

I need to talk about how it feels to be able to use computer sites, talk about AOL, and do some serious reading without problems, or backlash, or anger. And to do this without hooking into the things that come out of I am broke and I am alone and no one is doing anything.

AOL comes to my mind. They act like they have our good at heart, but they want to make money more than anything else.

As I write about it, I can feel it coming from my stomach and grabbing my throat so it feels kind of hard to swallow. I don't want to go there. I can't stop it.

I don't want it to come up. Shoot! I thought it was gone! Maybe it is like a seizure. If I mimic a seizure with my right hand, I can get into it and have one. Why do people put up with this [corporate greed?] And I am broken and I can't fix it. It overwhelms me.

It is the same kind of thing when I use a corporate site. I am angry that I can't talk to a person, and that I have to spend time getting this information for them to sell me something. I resent that! Why do people put up with this? And I am broken and I can't fix it. It overwhelms me. Son of a gun. I tapped into a feeling that wasn't there yesterday. Yesterday I just went there to get information. I wasn't angry or upset. I just wanted information and they had it.

As I was weeding my garden, I thought about my visit to the website of a national group fighting to defend Social Security. I signed up, saying I would come to a meeting, write letters, and go meet with my congressman when they needed me. It was the idea that I am connected enough to them to be of use, to be part of the army that they can call out when needed. I remember building that army for Welfare Rights, nurturing it, keeping people informed. It was good to think of the defense of Social Security being done on that basis.

I am willing to be part of a group working on an issue and then going home to work in my garden and enjoy my flowers. It is a matter of picking whom I can work best through. It's an ante up [apart] from just sending money, which I cannot do. But I can help on issues.

This is progress for me. When I was active before I went overseas, I didn't take time to relax. I could never do enough to justify stopping to rest.

For today, I'm just being happy with my yard and my flowers.

11:10 p.m.

The world is full of possibilities, and my relationship with Bob can be anything we want. It is wide open. So is the world. That feels pretty good.

Monday, May 2

11:00 a.m.

Had to get that little thought in last night, in case it left during the night, and also just because feeling so high at night is unusual! It's still here!

My body is already getting smaller. Harmony reigns in my mind. I want to explore having a functional body again with dancing and yard work and walking and yoga. A tiny bit of running!

I feel like I should be thinking about what I want to do with my life, what I want to work on. That is not what I want to do. I want to think about ballroom dancing classes, and ballet, and gymnastics. I want to get a solid base of enjoyment in my life before I worry about other stuff. It is pretty clear from the "broken" thing that my body started having seizures because it was the only way I could give myself a break. I don't know if they will stop now that I'm not broken anymore. There is a chance that it is hard-wired after all this time, so if I get overstimulated or overemotional my body will go into a seizure.

Among the other highs is the high I am feeling from having Bob in my life. He wrote something yesterday about the intense feelings when a new relationship starts. So it is not just me. That is good to know! And it is not defined as a particular form of relationship, despite the fact that the people around me assume this is some kind of love affair. It is some kind of connection. We are certainly full of delight in each other, but not a physical delight. I talked to him yesterday, and I am looking forward to seeing him again, to talking and cooking and making music together. And I'd like to trace the lines of his face with my fingers and touch his hands.

And then we got into a strange place in our email correspondence. The next part is a summary of the discussion we had.

May 2 And May 3

> M: We were talking about relationships, and I said the sex was always great, that that was the easiest part. You said it was due to the only constant, me. I blushed and grinned and am doing it again just thinking about it, but it did make me think.
>
> B: That's good, isn't it?
>
> M: My experience is limited in that I am always there. Rob asked me once if I didn't, in the middle of making love, just think how ridiculous this is and get out of the whole thing. I was totally amazed that such a thing could happen. It did help me realize that Rob and I would not be good together sexually, but it makes me wonder. And to wonder is to ask, when I at least am feeling like I'm in a totally intimate place with you.

For me, I am overwhelmed by it. The line from a poem about not knowing whether you have given or received a kiss is true for me. I am lost in feelings and desires and joy and lots of things, but I am certainly not engaged in normal, rational thought. I am beginning to believe that this is not true for everyone.

B: No. And it would probably scare a lot of people to feel as you describe. I agree with Rob. When you think that it's skin rubbing against skin and minds are going crazy over it? That's probably the reason why people tend to get embarrassed about sex. If you're not involved and you're observing more dispassionately, it can be ... maybe not ridiculous but at least ... funny?

M: Your reply totally stuns me. You agree with Rob. Wow. Do you mean this? I may have to rethink my whole life here! Let me rephrase here for clarification. You can think of sexual behaviors dispassionately as skin rubbing against skin. You do this easily when you are not involved, when your primary response is that it is funny-looking. When you are involved, it is a little harder to see the inherent ... silliness?... of the idea, but certainly possible.

Is that restatement true? Even vaguely true? You, when involved in making love, sometimes see it as a silly activity, concerning skin rubbing against skin, not worth all the brouhaha. Is that correct?

B: Yes. It makes a difference whether this is general or not.

M: Oh my goodness! Well, it certainly explains a lot of things, if most people aren't swept away but are at best thinking, "I wonder what she wants me to do?" or "Does he think my body is ugly?" [and] at worst, are thinking of lots of totally unrelated things. It challenges my whole view of sex to even think of rational thoughts going on...

B: There's a mix of irrational and rational, as in so many things. That seems normal, very human.

M: Are you speaking mostly in general terms, and not in specific? I want to know, specifically, about you and me and when we were lovers. It is full for me of such intense joy and celebration of each other, of being lost together, of being found together. I am not trying to be flippant or cruel or anything like that. I just know that what I have thought happened wasn't really happening if you were not there with me.

B: I am sorry that you're feeling this way. There are a lot of things going on with sex and our feelings and thoughts about it. We certainly don't all react to it in the same way, just as with anything else in life. That shouldn't make us sad, just maybe amazed at the diversity in human nature.

M: I'm sad because I have been just imagining so much in my life. What I thought was shared wasn't.

B: How do you know?

M: I know that it wasn't shared because you told me that it wasn't shared with you. And if it wasn't shared with you of all people, then whether it was ever shared is in doubt for me. When Rob talked of it, it had to be in general because we were never lovers. That made me realize the great differences there could be in how people make love and how they feel about it. Hearing you say that is very different, because you and I have been lovers, first lovers.

B: My point is that sex is very complex. People's attitudes toward it are very complex, usually more than they realize -- and definitely more than most would acknowledge to others. It all depends on the people and the circumstances and other factors.

M: I am asking about you, about your responses, your experiences. It's very disturbing coming from you because I thought that was where I learned it, where I learned how to go somewhere out of time and away from being alone to somewhere where the only thing that was happening was the wonder of us and the joy of being. I guess I made it all up, that it was just projection of how I felt onto something that wasn't that for you. What I felt as pleasure and love and acceptance at an overwhelming level coming from you was just a fantasy of mine. That makes me incredibly sad.

B: You are misunderstanding and exaggerating. I loved you. What we had was far more than physical. However, it was also physical. I am not trying to hurt you.

M: Knowing it was totally different for you will hurt me, but I didn't like knowing Santa Claus wasn't real; I got over it, and it had implications for my life. I know that you loved me. Was the physical separate from the love or an outgrowth of the love? Far more than the physical .... What does that mean to you?

B: We find evidence of the complexity and the extremes everywhere. We who believe in love, we who are romantic may have difficulty understanding or accepting that complexity, but it's there.

M: I am sorry to know that those of us who feel this as essentially a shared experience are often just deluding ourselves. A mystic's experience of contact with a higher power or saint is different depending on whether those powers or saints exist. Convince a mystic that it is chemical imbalance that causes the experience, and the whole thing becomes something different.

But there are poets and songs that celebrate this, and so I am not totally alone.

B: And you know that I've written a lot of poems and songs to celebrate love, including physical. So, even though I feel like you are lashing out at me now, I know that you don't believe that I think what you're accusing me of thinking.

M: I am sorry to be putting you through all of this! Maybe we have been talking at cross purposes this whole time. What is the truth for you is important. You have started me looking at many of the people who have been in my life, and viewing things in a different way.

B: When I point out the complexity of sex, you question me and you become upset. Sex is not intrinsically spiritual or emotional; it's physical.

M: My belief has been that the spiritual and emotional connection that I get when I make love is a real thing that is happening to two people. There are lots of levels to it, but for me, I am always totally in the experience, my rational mind is not functioning. You and Rob have convinced me that I am unusual in that respect. That is an incredible blow to my belief about my experiences in life. With that understanding, I can look again at things that I did not understand before, and look again at the things that I thought I did understand. Part of looking at things that I thought I did understand is looking at our relationship and what you felt when we made love. If I hold tight to this continuum idea, then your response does not need to break my heart. There may have been some reality in my thinking we were there together.

I'm just trying to understand here. It's hard because I have such strong feelings about this.

B: When we talk about rape, we can call it animal lust or a power play or whatever -- but we don't consider it spiritual or emotional. When we talk about some relationships, we recognize that it's more physical and less emotional or spiritual for one than for the other. That's not unusual. In fact, it seems perfectly natural.

M: If it is not overwhelming, what is it? Just kind of a nice thing to do once in a while?

B: For some people, at some times, with some people, it may not be overwhelming. For other people, at other times, with other people, it may be too overwhelming. Sex is not unlike food or alcohol or coffee or whatever things can be enjoyed or can be destructive or can lead to big disagreements between and among people or contribute to very wonderful experiences. And yes, poets and songwriters have celebrated food (I remember a poem from the 14th century about a melon!) and alcohol and probably coffee just as they have celebrated sex.

M: You were not there with me. That changes many things. That breaks my heart.

B: Please try to understand me. This is complex. Please don't simplify it.

M: I am filled with grief, with sadness, with loss. How can this be true? What in the world makes me so different? I've always thought so many incredibly different things, it would take a long time to list them all. I feel so alone! I just want to cry. I do not know exactly what is going on with me. I am confused, and sharing it with you. Not trying to lash out, just amazed at things.

B: I know you're not trying to lash out. Maybe I shouldn't feel that way.

M: Yes, complex, yes, different in place and time and person. I will try to understand your points and talk to you. Something major in my life has changed with this discussion, and it is not meant to hurt you. Be patient with me, please.

B: I'm patient. I'm just surprised that what I intended as a simple statement of a reality is affecting you this way. I'm sorry that it's making you sad and overwhelming you.

Tuesday, May 3

5:20 p.m.

Yesterday was an amazing day. I went to my meeting and physical therapy, loaded some stuff from the CD onto my computer and filed it all nicely. I downloaded Pandora and played with trying to get it to work. I messed with my yard some, talked to several people on the phone, and still had enough energy to go to the neighborhood meeting at night. Feeling wonderful.

Then came today, which for some reason has been really bad. I asked Bob if he got lost in sex and thought most people didn't. He, in effect, just said yes, which I thought meant he didn't. For some reason that kicked me off into a tizzy. It's one thing to lose the Catholic Church, which I did last week. Now my whole idea of what love was and whether you truly can connect with someone through making love seemed under attack. I felt like a freak. I feel like I weigh 30 pounds more than yesterday. I kept trying to make sense of this long discussion Bob and I were having and it just seemed to get worse.

One thing that bothers me about this whole "lost in sex" thing is what an idiot I am. I never doubted that most of the people I know would lose all rational thought and just be totally into it. I didn't understand the articles on how to please your man or knowing what your man wants, how to have a wonderful time, all the instruction. Didn't everyone just go with the flow?

It seemed that Bob shared my involvement, and if he wasn't really into it, wasn't really there with me, then no one ever was. Then I am a woman who thinks she is a mystic, seeing visions and connecting with God, when what is actually happening is I took a drug which produces these illusions. I wanted to believe that making love creates something wonderful.

But I don't see how it can when only one of you is lost in the experience and the other one is wondering what he's going to eat for breakfast tomorrow.

I know I'm being a little hard on myself here. But I feel like someone's pet dog who gets so excited about pulling on a rag, like it's totally important, while everyone else in the room is just into how cute the little dog is.

If I'm never loved, if I have never really been to the place I used to think Bob and I went to together, then there is no place that is so safe and happy, where I am accepted and part of someone else. It doesn't exist. There is nothing but me making up stories again, believing stuff that anyone with sense knows isn't true. I am tired of this!

I can still lose weight. I'm tired of being vulnerable if all I'm going to get is nothing but used for a while! Skin rubbing skin. I thought I knew something. Any woman who has had as many lovers as I have should know something, instead of just being a freak of nature that no one bothers to tell.

No one is going to read this but me. Maybe it will be different tomorrow; maybe I will learn something. I'm so sad that I've been half-crying, half-seizing all day, and I am so pissed at this second that I am worrying about busting the keys on the keyboard.

There is no one but me. There never was anyone but me. Maybe it was hormones or illusion or delusion. I don't want to talk to Bob about it anymore. I don't want to talk to anyone about it anymore. I just know that I never want to get lost in sex again by myself, with only my stupid little head and stupid little dreams. It's amazing that I am still alive. Jack off, you bastards. Seems the only thing I add to that is a softer mother-fucking spot for the activity, and less wear and tear on the hand. How could I even have said as much as I did to Bob? Here's my vulnerable little neck, feel like kicking it? Stomping on it? Or just playing with it and messing my head up?

And my first response to him is to try to make *him* not feel bad! Oh, thank you for destroying me, thank you very much. Did you hurt your boot when you stomped on my stomach? Sorry for being under your feet, sir! Why is *he* so important that if *he* doesn't believe in it then it never happened?

I think he was the best. He was the first, and it seemed so right and good and clean and overwhelming for me. But it was not much at all for him. I have no idea what it can be if it's not overwhelming. Nice? Interesting? Better than a cookie but not as good as an ice cream sundae? He compared it to food! Maybe I can eat it and think it is baked Alaska. That would be fun, wouldn't it? What is it if I'm all wrong? What can love possibly be about? No connection, just parts of the body momentarily satisfied? The only difference was me playing games in my head again? Like the black hole and all the other shit was just me playing games. Just games. Nothing real.

You are so fucking stupid! When will you ever get a clue about life? How can you have lived so long? It's good you never stayed more than six or seven years with someone. After a while they would have asked if you weren't tired of that game.

I don't like this. This is not fun. This is not good. I am so very sick of it. I want it to go away. But it just seems like I am too sad to let it go away. I don't understand it. I want to understand it. No, I want it to be the way I thought it was but it's not. It's not like that at all. It really is just people auditioning for the job of primary fuck partner. Like trying on clothing. Interchangeable body parts, but some of them feel a little better. Some of my body parts must have felt a little better to these people who stayed around. Is that love? Is that all it is? Some mediocre fondness for someone's body parts. It's not about people; it's about bodies and orifices. I was the one who had it all wrong. I was the one who didn't understand again again again againagainagainagainagain..... and forever. I am the one who just doesn't get it. Let me find a place all by myself and I won't talk to any of you people who understand everything so well ever again. Maybe you will leave me alone, little delusional idiot me who never never never never never seemed to have a clue about the rest of you and why you lived at all. I don't like how you live, but it beats, I guess it beats, making things up in your head.

Oh, God, he was saying that it's all just part of the variation. Does everybody just make things up in their head then? Is that what he was saying? Is that what he believes? Like on Halloween everyone dresses up, but I'm the only idiot who thinks I really am a pirate or a princess? I'm the only one who doesn't know it is a costume.

Why should I care so much about other people? Well, who the fuck is there but me and other people? I should just believe me? I can't just believe me!

Nova likes me. She doesn't think I am crazy. Oh, Nova, I can't do this, I can't let everything I have believed turn into little dreams in my head and float away.

Why the fuck are you crying again, you dumb bitch! You dumb whore who didn't know she was a whore. How stupid can you be? Do you ever think you will hit the limit? We are all tired of you; we want you to go away, you stupid girl who plays in her head and makes up stories. You go away and leave the rest of us alone. You get us into trouble all the time with your big ideas and fancy talking. SHUT UP with your goddam motherfucking nonsense, you bitch! You stinking dog in heat! Leave us alone.

Well, who the hell are you talking at me like that in my own head? Who are you saying that stuff to me? I try hard and I don't deserve this from my very own head! Stop it! Please stop it. I am tired. I want to rest. I want to be okay. I want I want I want I want I want endlessly and endlessly.

Why do you think anyone cares what you want? Do you have evidence for this, you stupid bitch? Tell us about it; we can destroy it. Tell anybody any of your little fragile things and they can destroy them. Don't you get it? Dog eat dog, and what the hell do you want to be — a little tiny bird who just gets to sing and fly around? The dogs will get you, and they will kill you, and they will play with you for a long, long time before you finally die, you stupid idiot who thinks that little birds should be allowed to live and fly and sing. Don't you know that bothers the dogs? They can't fly and sing. No one should be allowed to fly and sing. Don't you know anything?

I want to stop this but it just keeps going on. I am so sad and so tired. There's nowhere to escape. Come on, get a grip here. All you have to do is stop this. Stop typing, and then none of that stuff will come at you from the keys or from your head or from wherever it comes from. Oh, Nova, is this just another thing I can go through? The last bit in my head that is there to hurt me? Can it just be that?

And there I go, making things up again. I just make things up. Think of a rope to Nova. Hold on to the rope and you will be okay. But that is not real; I just made that up. Like my fantasy of love that I just made up. Like my fantasy of community that I just made up. Like I should live, which I just made up. Like anyone really cares.

Wednesday, May 4

5:45 a.m.

It's a new dawn! I feel so much better! Yesterday was the mother of all backlash days, and it is wonderful to have it over. I wrote four pages of attacks on myself, distilled into the one liner I sent Bob... "a bitch in heat with delusions of connection, who provided entertainment for a lot of people." I spent lots of time writing and rewriting and trying to get a handle on the meaning of my sexual behavior.

In the rambling, self-attacking pages, the "stupid" thing comes out a lot, as did the "I should have known better" stuff. The whole "why can't I be like other people" thing. Stuff from behind the wall. I finally started writing around 5:30 last night, and cried off and on the rest of the night. And smoked. And wrote. And had mild seizures. And had a pizza.

I was in loving relationships at times in my life. I was also in some totally screwed relationships. I put my whole sexual life into little boxes, and made up little stories to make myself feel better. The boxes fell apart and all the stuff merged and all the self-hatred came out. And I am here today. My eyes are still red from crying, my throat sore from seemingly endless cigarettes, but right now, in this moment, whatever I have done in the past does not matter. I'm alive and kicking. And the fact that I can do whatever I want, with whomever I want, in whatever way I want, is a joy. The past is the past.

It truly is a new dawn!

Friday, May 6

6:00 p.m.

Just another wonderful day!
I got my ticket to go visit Bob, which makes me smile. I wrote Rob yesterday, telling him about the sexual identity collapse and rebuild. I hadn't told him much since before Bob came to visit, and I was amazed at how much has happened since then. I didn't even tell him I wasn't a Catholic anymore! A lot is going on, but it feels like it is getting better and better.

Sunday, May 8

6:00 a.m.

Today is Mother's Day. I would be very surprised to see Jon today, less surprised to get a call. I expect not to hear from him at all. I find no impulse towards high drama today.
My son's presence or absence isn't a drama. I'm glad the feeling of being abandoned and unloved is just not there. My son is not central to my life anymore.
One of Phyllis's foster children, Anthonie, came over, and we had a good time, played badminton, watched a movie, had dinner. And then when he left, I couldn't stop thinking about Phyllis, critiquing her relationships with her children and foster children, thinking of everything she had done wrong and making her out to be the bad guy. I didn't attack Phyllis herself, didn't even really talk to her, but the venom was surprising.
Then last night was wonderful. I went out to put some cash in the bank, using the ATM machine at the corner store. I don't go out at night very often. It felt just like nights used to feel, somehow exciting and time for fun. I did some riding around and laughing, singing to the radio and listening to the loud noises my car can make. I need to find a dancing partner and go out at night. I don't feel secure enough to go by myself, but that may change. Meanwhile, there is at least one person I can ask, and maybe more than that. My own personal "Take Back the Night" celebration!

Monday, May 9

12:30 p.m.

A pretty strange thing happened yesterday. I spent hours outside working on the little flower bed. Maybe I was there too long. It must have been a dream I had of some gardening game and gardeners, whose voices kept hovering in my mind. I would try to snatch at them and the voices would disappear. It was like a dream that continues for a few seconds after you awake, but it went on longer.

Then Bob called, with a flood of awakenings. I tried to understand and think, but then just gave up and went with the flow.

I stayed in an odd place until I slept. When I awoke, I felt/still feel moved to a new and different place. Something has changed inside me. I do not know what yet, but I will watch and listen to myself. Or maybe I will never know exactly what happened.

Today it seems to me that the possibilities in my life have increased. I am having the time I talked about earlier, living in my house, in my neighborhood, just enjoying every day and what it brings. It is much easier to do than I thought it would be.

Tuesday, May 10

1:00 p.m.

I have lost enough weight that it is noticeable, and that causes me no panic at all. A little regret that I have to put up with men's approaches, but I get to move freely and stand tall and enjoy having a body. I can handle men.

My reading tastes have changed. I'm reading a Ralph Nader book and a couple of books on spiritual awakening and the psychiatric field.

I am not Catholic. I thought finding my political platform would be the next thing, but I think I need to focus on keeping contact with a higher power, and exploring that.

I am so ready to travel. I can even think about leaving Lansing. It would be a good time, since I'm changing so much and need to start some new things. I want to see Rob in British Columbia, and visit George and Rita in Florida.

I remain aware of the pages of shit I wrote about myself, all the self-hate, and am expecting to go over that with Nova. We may also want to look at what I know was a sexual awakening when I was 12 or 13 and my grandfather was after me.

Sounds like a lot of change and growth to me!

Wednesday, May 11

11:15 a.m.

Boy, what a confusing time for me! I think I've got a handle on things and then they fall apart. I am lucky to have people who can help me and whom I am learning from. Nova and I are spending much more time together and Bob is around now. Both are helping me.

We stand in our own way a lot. I let my preconceptions and what I thought I should do get in the way of looking at reality. Moving onto new ground is scary and pushes me towards old things.

Not being a Catholic changes some things about what I want to do with my life. The time with Bob let me see how totally valid relaxing and having fun can be. The total drive to constant work is gone, which is a relief! The idea that I am waiting to be "healed" so I can run away with the Catholics is gone. It leaves a hole.

I find myself resistant to finding different work in this town, which is one thing that makes moving appealing.

But if I have learned nothing else in this process, I have learned that change can be very rapid. I have to be patient. The thought of doing something else here makes me cry. I have so much history in this town, and I cannot seem to help comparing what I am doing with what I used to do. I have a lot of pride and a need to show people here that I can do important things.

I need to think about yesterday. I got up and it seemed like a wonderful idea to move to Monona so that I could see more of Bob. I would be close to my [program] sponsor Cathy, who lives near Chicago, and close to Chicago itself with all it has to offer. Jon doesn't see me or need me much at the moment; if everything is going to change, it would be easier to change in a new place. No one would have any expectations of me, so I could just find some part-time job if I wasn't able to work full time.

How much of that is a justification for trying to hurry the process with Bob? I went with that fantasy all day. Then it crashed last night, and I was so angry and upset with myself. I didn't want to look at it. I avoided writing about it. I could not stand the thought of having two of those crazy diatribes to read to Nova tomorrow. One is more than enough!

How much of an impact does the whole issue with my grandfather have? I have never talked to anyone about that, and my willingness to bring it up at this point amazes me. Did it scare me that it seemed to pop up out of nowhere? Tears are coming as I write this. Am I looking around real fast for a safe place?

I am so screwed! I don't know what I am doing, and don't know what I want to do. Except get better. But it is scary and I am alone, and I do not like that! Like the world cares. Oh, man, things are moving again. When will it stop?

I just checked back in the journal. The idea of moving, followed at the end by a little sentence kind of off-handedly mentioning my grandfather. Son of a bitch!

10:00 p.m.

What was I thinking? I went back and read all that shit, and more of it comes out. I just can't seem to stop it! I've been avoiding the keyboard, but it just comes. What do I think is so wrong with me? I try hard. I just want to be happy some of the time, and what is wrong with that? Why do I feel so bad?

I have to see Nova more often. This is just taking too long.

Why don't I deserve a decent man in my life? What is so wrong? Okay, you son of a bitch inside me, tell me about it. It involves me. I want to know.

It's not coming out. Instead I am just crying.

Why are you so mad at me? Please don't be so mad at me. Please don't hurt me. I am sorry for whatever I did.

Unfreezing Trauma

Oh, little girl, it is not you. You are okay. You just don't know very much. I am sorry, little girl. It is okay. You can rest. But what else is there with you? What is hurting you, little girl?

Oh, no, is it just so they will like you? Are you so worried they won't like you? You are okay; they don't matter all that much. You are okay, little girl. I am sorry we had to grow up. It was nice to be a little girl, but you can't stay there. You have to grow up.

You don't have to do things you don't want to do. You don't have to be with people who aren't nice to you. I don't want to make you talk. You don't have to talk if you don't want to. Nobody is going to do anything bad to you. It is okay, it is okay, it is okay.

You didn't do anything wrong, little girl. You were trying to be good. You don't have to let anyone do anything to you.

Is this all about being liked? Oh, my god, that is so wrong. That is bad. You don't have to do that, little girl.

I am sorry that bad things happen to you. It is not okay that things get so bad and you get so lost. Oh, my god, it is my little girl who is lost and confused in all of this. Oh, you poor little girl! It is okay. It is grown-up stuff. It can be okay. It is not always about bad things. It is not always. You are okay, little girl. Don't cry so much, little girl. Oh, my little girl, don't cry. It can be all good; every part of it can be good. You don't have to cry. You don't have to save anyone. You don't have to please any one or make them happy. If I want to, I will do that; I will do those things that confuse you so much. Oh, my god, my little girl has been the one. You poor little girl! You lost your helmet and you are so sad.

I am not mad at you, little girl. I didn't know it was you I was yelling at. I am sorry I scared you. You are a good little girl, but you are so little and so young. You weren't supposed to have to learn about men until you were big like them, and then you would have liked all of it. You don't have to hide. You don't have to do anything.

You are safe. You are okay. I won't yell at you anymore. I didn't know it was you. I didn't know you were so scared. Some of the men didn't know it was you and didn't know you were scared and lost. They didn't know either; so many of them are sorry too, and the other ones, the bad ones, they won't get you. You will be okay.

The baddest man is gone. He can never come back to get you. He will never get you again. He can't. He's dead, little girl, and you are here and you are safe.

Oh, you poor baby! You didn't have to make him happy with you. You didn't have to do that, but I know you wanted everyone to be okay and you thought it was your job and it was very confusing for you. Your body felt so strange. It wanted things that were not nice. You wanted things that felt good and felt bad at the same time and it was too much for you. But you are okay now. It is okay now. You can be okay now.

It is okay for big people who love each other and want to do that and it doesn't feel bad to them at all. It is not bad for them. It was bad for you. It was not good for you at all. It was not your fault that you didn't know what to do. It was a hard thing to know what to do and no one ever told you about it, besides all the people who said it was always bad. They didn't tell you that sometimes it felt good, and that sometime you would know that it was just good and right and that time would come, but it wasn't the right time for you. It just was not your time yet.

You don't have to hide from me. You don't have to hide anymore. You have some people who will still like you. Oh, my god, how could it be about being liked? How could it be? You don't have to make bad people like you. Momma would have understood. She wouldn't have been mad at you if you told her, but you didn't know. It's bad, but it is not your fault. It was not your momma's fault; she couldn't have known.

But why didn't someone know? He was always touching me, touching me, touching me again and again and soft and soft and soft until my body wanted things, but I was so confused. It wasn't right and I knew it wasn't right but I didn't stop him. I might have been able to stop him. I promised myself I would stop him from stroking, stroking, stroking me until I didn't know what I wanted. I got lost in feeling, lost in the feelings, lost in the feelings, just lost there with the good and the bad all mixed up. I want someone to love me, but not that way, not the mix, just the good, but I can't have the good because the bad is always there, always there.

I don't want it to be there. It is not just a mistake when the bad isn't there; sometimes it is just good. You don't have to keep waiting for the bad to come back. We are smarter now, little girl. We can pick people and we can pick the ones who are good. And it is okay: we deserve the good. We are not bad, little one; we just try to be good and get better. That is all. It is okay. But I am tired of doing this by myself

I am tired. I am very, very tired and I want to go to sleep. Nova will come tomorrow and we will ask her to come faster next time so you won't have to hide and wait and cry and worry. But even if she can't, I will know it is you and I will not yell at you so much. I am sorry I was so mean and called you bad names. I should have known it was you, but I didn't. I was surprised, but you are okay now, you are okay. All the bad things are over and we will try really hard not to let the bad things come, because you do not deserve the bad things, you do not deserve the mix, just the good.

You can have the good. You are not the bad, and the bad doesn't have to be part of it at all. You are okay. You can rest. You can sleep. I am so sorry, little girl. I did not understand.

Thursday, May 12

6:30 a.m.

I slept last night imagining the little girl in my arms and Bob on the couch nearby. I was safe.

What a surprise it was! Some of the beginning got lost when I hit a wrong key because I was crying so hard I couldn't see the keyboard. This negative stuff had been hounding me all evening – "you don't deserve a good man" kind of shit – but I didn't want to go there, didn't want to let it come out on the keyboard. I even varied the way I walked through the dining room so I wouldn't be close to the computer. Finally I decided I had enough strength to fight it out with that voice and went in blazing, cussing, hollering. And then came my little girl, crying, asking me to please stop. It came out in a rush; it was coming so fast and I was so upset and I was trying to keep up with it all.

Black and white. That is all my little girl can see, good or bad, not even any variations on those words. That son-of-a-bitch grandfather of mine, to arouse a child who in her life is still hitting boys who say they like her! I was so not ready for that, so confused about it all. And that has been following me, has been a part of my sexuality ever since. No wonder I picked losers so often. During the celibate years after the divorce, the top talk in my mind was all about not needing or wanting a relationship, when underneath was all the stuff about messing up. My little girl saying, *"You are a bad girl, bad, bad, bad. You do bad things and you should be sad and by yourself because you are different and you are bad."* Right underneath, where I couldn't hear, where I just felt.

It is odd but interesting to hear from different sides of me. Not so separate anymore. They are talking to each other. Maybe my body and emotions will talk so much that the seizures can stop. That would be amazing!

My sponsor Cathy just called. She didn't think I was crazy to consider moving to Monona. I didn't think she'd say that. I'm really just playing with pluses and minuses of the area. There isn't anything totally out of the ordinary about that. People move.

We get to cover two weeks tonight; talk will be mostly sex, I think. Was it really just an innocuous statement from Bob that kicked this all into gear? Yesterday I reread the trash pages and it started hollering at me. Again

You got my attention, little girl.

10:30 a.m.

It was hard sitting in the [12-step] meeting this morning. Things were just popping away.

One thing that hit me is how circuitous my thinking has had to be! I think the whole fixation of making amends to Bob for what I did to mess him up and contribute to his habit of putting up with bad treatment from women is a strange path to being okay to be with him. If I look at how I have harmed him, I can think of our relationship as a bad thing in some way. If it is bad, the resistance to the relationship decreases. What an odd path to take!

The pathways from one thing to another have had to go around some fairly weird fixed thinking. I am building more straight paths in my brain. As the blocks from trauma and life lessons misunderstood are removed, things can move more freely. I am lucky to have people whom I trust, and who are smart enough to help me with this.

I am getting a feeling of closure about many things. Closure with working at the community college. I think I am ready to leave. Closure with Jon, to let him lead his own life and make his own mistakes. Even closure with my house. Most of my plans for it have come to fruition, and I am happy with it. I'm feeling good and able to move on.

I was thinking about my ex, Tommy Walker as well. He was a lost soul, too. Driven in some ways by guilt. We were driven by the dual good-bad thing throughout our relationship. We shared in some way the same demons. Driven by the desire for good things, and held back by the belief that we deserve bad things. I wish I could have helped him more, but I couldn't even help myself at that point. I hope he is joyful wherever his spirit is. It feels like something is finishing with him as I write this.

SESSION ELEVEN

Friday, May 13

All we did last night was read. And cry. We didn't talk much.

Nova had some interesting comments. I got angry when she interrupted my reading the long conversation with Bob, being logical. It was not a logical thing. I was circling the issues and had to drag her through the whole thing. She said all I wanted was her to witness.

She also said my describing being totally lost while making love was the ideal for many. I hadn't thought of that. I was focused on people knowing I was abnormally overwhelmed by sex and using that against me.

I could not believe the length of the conversation with Bob about being lost in sex. Nova wondered why he didn't get angry. I asked. He answered. I didn't believe him. I asked again in different words. He answered. I still didn't accept it. On and on. What I saw as his endless patience Nova saw as abuse. Or was she talking about my treatment of him when we were lovers? He was so solidly good, so wonderful, that I ran away to get the bad because the bad had to be there.

Why did he tolerate me? I am beginning to see the whole thing as pretty complex for both of us. I was so angry at him for not telling me I was a freak, an abnormality. But how would he have known? I was his first as well.

I know what I tell people in recovery. That they don't have to finish everything right away, that there is time to deal with things, and sometimes it is just time to note them and to move on. This may be the time to do that. Maybe it is time to read more and think about broad things before delving into the particulars again. I need to rest and learn some things.

We aren't going to meet again for two weeks. But I will be on vacation with Bob, so I won't be journaling much. I want to take a break, but I am afraid I will lose things. That is why I write them down.

It feels more like a start than an end. It's the thing with my grandfather. It is not over. I can't believe how quickly I passed over it the day after the "little girl lost" thing, like it was settled.

NOVA'S COMMENTS ON SESSION ELEVEN

We didn't do EMDR at this session. We didn't have time! Mary had been through so much in the intervening two weeks. Her immense anger at Bob for his temperate analysis of love, her terrible feelings of humiliation, "the only one who was lost in love," I would have expected her to value her ability to have such feelings. She saw herself as an object of ridicule, "somebody's pet dog who gets so excited pulling on a rag, like it's totally important, while everyone else in the room is just into how cute the little dog is." And then she goes into a rage, and she was in a rage, on paper and in person, weeping with shame and embarrassment. And after the torrent of rage and vilification, she ended with a list of things—"I just made up!...a fantasy of love, a fantasy of community, ... like I should live, which I just made up!" What doesn't fit in that line? She should have said something like "the brotherhood of man" to end the statement. But she said "like I should live, which I just made up" The secret we were pursuing suddenly showed its face.

I didn't interpret this, I would like to announce at once. I just watched and listened and wondered what is happening?

INTERVAL ELEVEN

Saturday, May 14

9:00 a.m.

I spent time walking and thinking yesterday.

When I put it in terms of another person living inside me, my little girl, it makes sense that she is the one who is always in control when I have sex. I can talk about her conflicts, the good and the bad, how she dives into the whole mess. In reality it is just me.

I don't know where to go from here. If I look at the things that make me cry and squirm and want to run, or at the two nights of meltdown, it's anger at men and the experience with my grandfather all mixed up in my sexuality. In being used. I don't know what I can pull out of that for EMDR. These two weeks have been really painful.

I still have a feeling it is dangerous to concentrate too much time on the idea of my little girl, talking to her and treating her like a different person from me. I think of peace as the absence of all the competing thoughts inside me. When I experience peace now, am I just suppressing or are they moments of integration? This feels good and is recent in origin. It is connected with nature, with my garden, with walking in the city, and noticing the natural world. Talking to my little girl and the other voices inside has been the primary way for me to access things that are really buried deep inside.

I want to spend time comforting my little girl who was so totally overwhelmed and confused by the sexual responses her grandfather produced. He would go on for what felt like hours to my child, stroking near my breasts, or he would have his hands moving slowly back and forth nearer to my genitals, not reaching there but millimeters closer on each repetitive stroke. This usually happened in his living room on the couch, where we would all be watching TV. I would get to the point where I could feel the moisture, the vagina readying for penetration, though I did not know what it was at that time. I remember leaving for the bathroom, which was off his bedroom. He whispered to me "Are you getting wet?" He knew what was happening to my body. I didn't know how he knew that, but it felt wrong, and scary.

He seemingly could not contain himself as he neared the erogenous zones. Once he had me in my parents' bed (how did he manage that?) and he made a lightning attack on my clitoris. I fought, escaped, and ran. Another time I was sick in bed in the basement bedroom. I don't know how he scared me that time, but I had to get away. I dragged myself away, up the stairs, and fainted in the kitchen. I have a split-second memory of another time, his trying to grab Anna and me in his kitchen, fighting him together and winning.

He tried French kissing when we visited him. Or he would slip a $100 bill or a $20 into my bra. I told my mom he had given me some money, but not how.

I remember the little vibrator he had, with straps for attaching to his hand. It made his hand vibrate, and he used it on me. I think it happened often, but I don't remember all the times. Once he had me in his bed and somehow my breasts were exposed. He went for them with his vibrating hand. I remember being terrified.

I will not go into this more until I have a session with Nova. That will be less painful than what I have been going through.

Meanwhile, I will try to be nice to my little girl. I have promised her that we will not have sex until she is okay, that we will not get into situations which will take us there. I will also not go after her again. She is such a source of all these things, and she is little, and she is scared and tired and has been working very hard for a long time.

I think I have enough stuff to move ahead for a while.

I am going to concentrate on my poor little body, which has suffered so much in all of this. I am going to dance and sing and walk and stretch and look around as I do. That is the focus as well, not how am I going to change the world or what am I going to do with my life, but how can I enjoy this body and help it get better.

Stronger. Healthier and happier. That will make my little girl happy. Making amends to myself. It is a strange world.

Sunday, May 15

5:15 a.m.

I've been walking a lot the last few days, and yesterday I consciously took my little girl on a walk with me. She was not so interested in the flowers, but liked the mud puddles, the playground, and the people.

We talked and reached an agreement. I promised her I would not attack her any more. I need a new way to uncover things, other than the armed-and-hunting thing I did last week. At first I was just seeing it as painful, and I wanted to avoid pain. But it was an actual attack on myself, on my little girl, and that cannot be tolerated. I will not attack myself.

The last session was so strange for me, and I think for Nova as well. I may call her today and tell her that I now have some targets for EMDR and have made a decision to try a different method of uncovering things.

I am quiet and contemplative today. It has been a while since I have read much of anything that was challenging, but I have started *The Cosmic Game* by Grof, a book that Rob recommended.

I am feeling confident about finding my own way with the help of friends. I am thinking of working at the community college as a necessary interruption to what I am doing. I have to pay the bills while I am getting better. Finding something to wear to work may be a problem; it feels like the weight is just falling off. I do not want to be there in the fall, but I have some minimal hours scheduled if that becomes necessary.

But the main focus is growth in two areas: working on the things I have identified through EMDR and working on my body. I promised my little girl that I would work on being able to run. The only other thing I am conscious of at this point is the black-white, good-bad mind set. It is very simplistic, and I fall into it a lot. My little girl makes that very clear, but it is not confined to her. I don't know the source of that; it may just be the result of not thinking deeply for a while. But I am not going to try to track it down brutally.

I miss Bob already; he is going on a trip, and he will be out of touch. I do get [to] go there to see him this week after he gets back from his trip, and I am excited about that. It is tempered by the knowledge that this weekend trip he is making may result in some resolution to his relationship with his long-distance girlfriend, either continuing it or ending it. I don't know which will be better for them in the long run. It may just be continuing what is unsatisfactory. My little girl likes him, too.

Monday, May 16

7:05 a.m.

What shit I write about Bob. What I want to want for him. I do really want him to be very happy. I also want him to be most happy with me, and for there to be a place where this relationship can go in terms of romance.

I have to stop all that kind of thing. I was so into worrying about him and trying to convince myself I don't have a strong interest in him as a possible mate. Certainly at this point in time, I need to try to tell the truth! Things are changing too much to try to simultaneously decide what I really believe and impose on myself what I want to believe. I have to stop being dishonest with myself in the journal because he will be reading it.

Yesterday was strange. I got up at 2:30 a.m. worried about Bob. Generalized worry. Going all the way to worry about whether his plane will crash. I was so tired when I finally went to my [12-step] meeting that I could hardly pay attention, and didn't get much out of it.

I wanted to be in a different spot, but couldn't see how to get there. Then Phyllis called. She had tickets to a play and did I want to go? I said sure, and two hours later we went to see 110 Degrees in the Shade.

And in the middle of watching it, I thought how much fun it was to be in a play, and remembered plays I had been in. I could learn how to dance and do the kind of thing they were doing. I could be in the chorus right now, maybe someday stop smoking and work on my voice and play the lead. I could do anything!

If I follow the trend in my family, I might live to be 85 or so. That's over 30 years to go! That's a long enough time to do just about anything.

As they sang about night being the magical time, and talked about just believing in your dreams and following them, I thought about all the things I have been and done already. About how much I have told Bob and focused on the bad things, how I have been thinking of my life as a series of traumas and strange decisions, bad times, bad things.

I have done a lot in my life! Sure, the years since 1994 have been a battle to function. But I was around for 44 years before that! I did many things. It is not so blank.

Bob has a better idea of all the things that have been wrong in my life than anyone besides Nova. He knows of traumas and thoughts that no one else does. But unlike Nova, he knows almost nothing about all the successes in my life, all the fun and exciting and wonderful things I have done. How skewed his idea of me must be! And how skewed my idea of myself has been!

One of the people in the play was really cynical, really dismissive of the people around him, wanting them to "live in reality," which meant accepting lots of limitations that may be partially true, but were not totally true, and could be changed with work and attitude. I told Phyllis that we were like that. When I am with Phyllis, it is easy to fall into that same place. We are powerless, our lives are almost over, and all we can do is talk bad about people.

What I see is that she has given up on life and is just waiting to die.

I talked about how having Bob back in my life made me realize how much I was when I met him, and times when the world was wide open to me, and I was just learning all about it. Excited, enthusiastic. How much things have changed as a result of that and of EMDR.

I feel an obligation to try to reach her before I go. It seems clearer to me all the time that I want to go, and am readying myself to go. I'm not sure where. I am thinking of concentrating on myself, of getting my body better, of working through all the weirdness that lives in my mind and finding a new basis of spirituality, not saying my life is over and I am stuck here forever!

Tuesday, May 17

10:20 a.m.

I spent a lot of yesterday reading some more of the Grof book. I am excited about where I will go on a spiritual basis now that I am not a Catholic, and probably not a Christian. It is not an option to not have a spiritual life. Bottom line is I cannot stay sober without a power greater than myself; I don't back up from that. I remember too well what it used to be like, and I never want to go back there. Sometimes I am remembering exactly what it was like, exactly how it felt to be at the point where I had to decide whether to accept that I was going to be a drunk for the rest of my life and try to figure out how to end it, or if I could be willing to admit the possibility of the existence of some power in the world that would help me not drink. It was a hard choice, made very tentatively, but it worked.

I have talked to many people in the [12-step] program who take offense or feel singled out for criticism by what other people say at meetings. I have been amazed when they say that, for I never feel that way unless they refer to me by name. Then I know they are talking about me.

This morning the guy who talked soon after I did talked about cursing, and how he can't hear the message for the cursing. He went on about how he cursed twice last week, and it told him he was not in good spiritual condition. Someone who talked after him mentioned the "s" word. Shit? That's cursing?

When I am totally in today, I watch my language. I started this when Jon's stepchildren were spending time with me. Substituting "Holy Moly" for "son of a bitch," "oh my goodness" for "oh my God". I pay attention to what comes out of my mouth.

I don't do that when I am revisiting or remembering strongly what it used to be like. I'm sure the "motherfuckers" were flying this morning. I think he was talking about me! I wonder if my language is going to be changing all the time even when I am feeling in a different spot. It affected me, and I tell my sponsees when someone says something that they react to it because part of them believes it applies to them. I feel he was criticizing my language. It is uncomfortable. When I revisit times in my life, the language that I use seems to change as well. I don't know if I can stop that or want to stop that. I just feel strange.

The belief that I limit myself is growing so strong, and the feeling of endings and new beginnings is very strong. I really do not know what role Bob will play in this. I do not know if I am in fact going to move from this place, but I do know that my life is changing at an incredible rate and I have to maintain my openness.

Amazing stuff. Life is full of amazing stuff.

11:45 a.m.

Just finished my yoga routine, and I am feeling wonderful. I am unable to balance at all on my toes. I am working on it, but it is part of my routine that I have trouble with in various postures.

But that is not the reason I came here. I wanted to stress again for myself the need to give up the "want to want" to believe things, and just try to find out what I believe. The "want to want" comes from the first time I took the second step. I want to want to believe that I can stop drinking. At that point it was a positive thing. I was so caught by alcohol, it was such a power in my life, that the tentative step towards believing it was possible to be sober was the best I could do.

But I am past that point, and it is necessary for me to try to just tell the truth. I need to tell the truth to Bob as well, which is really tricky. But if I don't, it will morph into something else. My mind has so many ways to keep me from growing towards the light. It is appealing to think that our relationship is limited by a current commitment he has. He would have to end his relationship with his long-distance girlfriend. A part of me really wants that. Another part of me hears the pain in his songs and in his voice, and I want him to be happier. I want some resolution of this thing with her that will bring him a period of joy, either with her or without her. The temptation, the false pathway, is for me to convince myself that

I am somehow committed to a long-term relationship with him, that I know what should happen with us. I can play unrequited love or something like that. Most of the people around me, the people at meetings, Beth and Phyllis, all think that it is a love affair, and that is all. But I know that the glow and smiles are from the excitement of spiritual growth and understanding as well as Bob, and that I do not know what should happen in the future. Predicting will limit it.

I woke this morning with distaste for sex and some understanding that it is a peculiar looking activity. That seems funny to me at this second, but it is part of being okay with a continuum. I am also drawn by the fact that in Grof's book, he speaks of sexual union as being a way of spiritual growth.

Wednesday, May 18

10:30 a.m.

Just got a note from Bob, and things went well with him. I am glad he is okay, but I'm not too sure about me! My eyes sparkle when I talk about him; I can't stop that. I don't know what it means, but I need to be careful. No more doomed relationships. I'm going tomorrow. A friend from my morning [12-step] meeting is seeing me off at this end, and Cathy is picking me up in Chicago, and there are meetings right by Bob's house. I will have plenty of help staying in the moment. He is so solidly there as well that he is a help in this process. He will help me figure out how we can be in each other's lives.

I continue to lose weight, and it continues not to scare me. I consider spirituality that is totally different than anything I have experienced before, and I am willing to continue looking. I am taller, my house is bigger, and I am planning on living 30 years more. I am changing.

I started this morning feeling like I deserved to be punished. I was hoping I didn't have to track that down after the meeting. At the meeting we read something about taking personal inventory daily, that it may seem like wasted time but it isn't.

I almost laughed. Far from being a waste of time, it is the best use of time! I have given myself such a great gift. Since I started EMDR and stopped working, I have been doing hours of work on myself every day. For almost two months I have been on a self-created retreat. Meetings six times a week, with daily writing and examination of myself, often pushed by things that happen in the meeting. It's grown to include yoga and walks. I have been sharing what I write with Bob on a daily basis, and going over it with Nova regularly. How lucky I am to have the daily support I need, and the money that amazingly seems to be lasting!

Giving myself this time of prayer and meditation and reflection and self-discovery is the best thing I could do. It was long in the simmering, but like a pudding, it has hit the critical point and is thickening in front of my eyes. I just have to go along with it and let it all happen.

But I have to admit it is scary, that I can run away with the whole Bob thing. I have to be careful not to set myself up.

Thursday, May 26

10:30 a.m.

It's been a week since I wrote. Last week at this time, I was on the train to Chicago. What a week it has been!

I noticed this morning that I have been feeling it is my fault for having seizures. Noticing the absence of that feeling. It is not my fault. I did not do anything wrong. Some things happened to me and I did the best I could. Now is the time to move on from there. It took me almost 28 years of being sober to go where the dragons are, to head my little boat straight for the dragons, and with Nova and Bob in my boat and the people in my meeting behind me, to just see what the heck lies in that direction. The topic this morning was "launching your boat in sobriety," and I know that I have launched my little boat in a new direction.

It is not that bad. It will not kill me to go there and look at it all. I will not go to the black place; I will not have to kill myself. Regardless of what happens, I do have a life and I will continue to have a life. It might not be what I expect and it is certainly not what

I thought of when I was a child, but it is a life, my life, and it will be okay.

Part of that is true and part of it is what I want to be true. I want to be there. I want to believe that. It may not be my fault for being here, but the fact is that I feel pretty useless.

That is the theme I share with Cathy. We both tend to define ourselves by what we can do, and what we can do is so limited at times. She's had a kidney transplant, and her diabetes is not under very good control. Like the people in my life are used to my seizures, her family is used to calling the paramedics to come get her. She can't work. I look at her life and see how much she gives just by being who she is. How important she is to her husband and her boys, to me, to the people around her in recovery, to the woman she is teaching English and to that woman's family, the whole network she is part of. It's not how much she can work that is important.

It is harder to give myself that same break. It is not about how much I can do. I don't really believe that totally or even partially. I don't feel broken if I am unable to deal with the world. I am still okay with that, which is kind of amazing. I can deal with it.

But I still feel like I have no place in the world of work, that I am not really needed very much. Do I have to be totally needed to justify my own existence?

I have not gone very far into what I think of as my new journey in spirituality, but it seems to me to be the clue at the moment. I notice that I am wearing more of my necklaces. Since I am not a Catholic, I don't wear the cross all the time. That is an outward sign to me of a change in attitude.

I am part of a network. I hope to grow in my understanding of it. I want to become more aware of it. It is the materialist universe, the idea that we are what we do and earn and attain in a material sense, that makes me feel useless. In a spiritual sense I am more than that. I am part of other people and they are part of me. Together we get through this journey in the rough times and enjoy this journey in the good times. I can relax and know that I am not alone.

This seems right as I follow it.

If my calendar is correct, I will be seeing Nova tonight. I want to do EMDR on my grandfather. I have a particular scenario in mind. I want to come out of it really believing that I am not dirty and sick and evil when I am sexually aroused. Natural desires are natural. He was wrong to do that to me. I was overwhelmed and confused. I want to feel that I can fall in love and make love and that it can be totally wonderful. I want my little girl to feel clean and healthy and natural, not dirty and bad.

Negative cognition: I am dirty and bad and unclean and unworthy of love.

Positive cognition: This one is harder. I did the best I could? I can forgive myself? I have nothing to forgive? That last one doesn't seem right. Nova talks about [the positive cognition] being the opposite [of the negative cognition]. How about "*I am clean and good and worthy of love*"? That's negating all the words, and I don't believe that one at all! Is it possible to get there?

Monona and Madison, where I visited Bob, was so pretty and clean that I felt like I didn't deserve to be there, wasn't capable of functioning there. All those clean, useful people, capable people, with strong bodies. If I don't even believe I deserve to be in beautiful surroundings, how can I believe I am worthy of love? Seems like light-years apart to me. But there were times when I felt it was okay that I was there.

I have such strange thoughts. They are very sad thoughts. I cry as I write them.

As I look back at what I have written, it seems very disjointed. It is the best I can do right now.

SESSION TWELVE

Friday, May 27

Before the session I looked at the journal to see what I have written. I could hardly believe I had actually written all that stuff about my grandfather. But there it was, so I had to read it.

Start of Session
Negative Cognition: I am dirty and bad and unclean and unworthy of love. Belief: Highest on scale

Positive Cognition: I am clean and good and worthy of love. Belief: lowest on scale, totally disbelieve

It didn't take too long. I concentrated on the scene in my head. I am in the living room at my grandfather's house, and my grandfather and I are sitting on the couch with a blanket over us. Other people were around.

It seems I only watched her fingers for a minute and then I started screaming. It was my little girl and she shouted, ***"BAD MAN! HE WAS A BAD BAD BAD MAN! HE SHOULD NOT HAVE TOUCHED ME! HE SHOULD NOT TOUCH LITTLE GIRLS!"*** It went on and on for over an hour, I think, screaming and crying and calling him a bad man, pounding on the table with all my might, imagining it was him.

At one point my heart broke when I heard my little girl say, *"I have to keep him from the littler girls. I can stand it."* My poor little girl: she thought she could stand anything.

At another point, I got real mad at St. Maria Goretti. She got stabbed 31 times or some horrible number rather than let a man touch her. I said she was a bad girl.

Think how much she hurt her mother and brothers and sisters. She was not smart; she was just dead! That was not good. She should have let him; she didn't win, she was dead, and everybody was very sad, and it was HER FAULT. She wasn't a saint; she was bad!

Nova thinks I had to stop being a Catholic before we could get to this, and that I had to find my little girl behind the wall before we could get to this.

Little bursts of thoughts and then the screaming, *"He was a bad man. Somebody should have beat him up. I could beat up the little boys who tried something, but he was a big man. He was A BAD BAD BAD BAD MAN! I wish he were alive so I could kill him, so I could beat his face in. HE WAS A BAD BAD BAD MAN WHO SHOULD NOT TOUCH LITTLE GIRLS!"* I screamed as loudly as I could, my voice hoarse, stopping at one point to put my face on the table and sob. I would be calmer for a second and feel like an adult, and then my little girl was back and screaming some more.

During a lull, we tried to finish. We knew it was not done, and decided to do it again next week.

End of Session

Negative Cognition: I am dirty and bad and unclean and unworthy of love. Belief: still highest on scale

Positive Cognition: I am clean and good and worthy of love. Belief: belief has gone up a little.

I was exhausted and went to bed almost right away. I lay there patting my shoulder, telling my little girl that she was okay, rocking her and trying to comfort her.

NOVA'S COMMENTS ON SESSION TWELVE

In Interval Eleven, Mary starts with some details about her grandfather, but then discusses this, that and the other, with only two short references to the subject we would have to deal with next, grandfather. The EMDR session did not expose and analyze Mary's feelings of guilt about her reaction to her Grandfather's attempt at seduction. What happened was an explosion of rage and indignation that she should have suffered all this time when it was HIS fault! He was a bad, bad man. He should never have touched her! And St. Maria Goretti, she might be pleased with herself, getting to be a saint by taking on 31 dagger blows. But did she think of her family? Did she think how sad she was making her mother? In a few sentences little Mary repudiated her long-held feeling of guilt and rejected her passionate aspiration to receive the glory of sainthood. " *She was not smart. She was just dead. That was not good. She should have let him. She didn't win. She was dead, and everybody was very sad and it was HER FAULT. She wasn't a Saint, she was BAD.*"

But, of course, it couldn't be this easy. An hour and a half of screaming fury at this unreasonable burden would not erase the years that Mary had accepted and carried her burden. She faced another pain-filled week.

INTERVAL TWELVE

Friday, May 27

5:30 a.m.

> excerpt *from email to Bob.*
>
> I had a difficult time calming down last night, and thought of you. I tried to envision you on my couch here, but ended up being at your house with you in the sound studio. It was comforting
>
> We hit the mother lode of rage last night. I screamed long after I was hoarse from screaming, and pounded the table and cried for maybe two hours. Nova did some eye movement things to bring me to a safe place. I'm not going to journal on this; I don't want to go back there by myself. We will continue on the same topic next week. The stuff with that bad man went on longer and involved more things than I was aware of. It's okay to repress this for a week more. My fear is that it will jump back out, so I won't go there.
>
> It can be scary out in the world, alone in our heads. I think being totally alone is a choice. I do not apologize for wanting you to hold my hand, or even just hold me, while I cry and try to rest. You are very important in my life right now. I am not alone, and you are one of the people with me. If I were all alone, if I were by myself, I would have nothing to stop me from knowing what I know, that I must die.

11:00 a.m.

excerpt from second email to Bob

I cried all through my morning 12-step meeting and am angry at him right now. I think a lot of things will fall into place when this is done. I know that it will be done but it sure isn't done yet!

I'm afraid of getting lost in the stuff that came up last night, so I called Nova and she will be here around noon. Hope it works! I spend all this time getting stuff to come out, and now that it is out I can't seem to put it away very well. As soon as I relax the slightest in my head, all of this stuff comes, the "bad man" stuff, then the "I should be dead" stuff comes, and I will be so sad and I will have to do it. I have to keep putting it away every second — put it away, I will think about it later.

I am going to eat lunch and play on the computer until Nova gets here. Those are my plans. I have to concentrate just on my plan and make it through the next little bit of time until Nova gets here.

Thanks for all the help.

9:30 p.m.

This is the longest I have waited to write about a session. It was hard to get to the point where I wrote down the stuff we talked about last night, and then to actually talk about it. I had not talked to anyone about it in my life, besides a quick "My grandfather sexually molested me, no problem" on a medical history sheet. It wasn't quite that easy.

When I got up this morning it was still there. It was like the memory had come back and I couldn't make it go away again. It was like the frozen memories of all the other stuff, but I had to work very hard to even get to this frozen memory, and now I don't know what to do with it! I went to my [12-step] meeting, cried, and didn't say much. But in the car my little girl was pounding the steering wheel, screaming, "*BAD BAD BAD BAD BAD BAD MAN!!!*"

I called Nova when I got home. I couldn't do anything but think about it and be sad or angry. Nova came and I don't remember if we did any EMDR or if she just talked to me about victims and old men who prey on young girls; that it was natural to get aroused, a good thing but not the right time and not the right person. She said how hard it is for a child in that situation to know what is going on. Adults know what is going on, but children do not, and they can't protect themselves.

I felt better and my little girl is not in charge of me now. We aren't going to scream and yell and holler at him now. We will save that; we are not finished.

I stayed in the house all day, but just went out now to deposit some money. I cried in the car, but not the loud wail of the little girl, just the soft cry of me at how sad [that] it happened. I kept it secret for many years. And now the secret is out, and Nova says I am a good girl and I did good and I am not bad. I want to believe her, and maybe I will. I believed her for a while today.

No wonder it felt like men were always nipping and pulling at me.

Saturday, May 28

4:30 p.m.

excerpt from email to Bob

It got very bad last night after I wrote you and I cried a lot and it was just not good.

It was very nice to get a letter from you letting me know that it was okay. You said you were proud of me for having the courage and the strength to go through this. And I have to thank you very much for that. I sometimes feel very alone and like I am not doing a good job here.

10:20 p.m.

excerpt from email to Bob

It was great talking to you, just what I needed! I felt like I was at the festival with you. Madison and Monona look better every day. You are such a lot of fun to be with! I would love for you to come here again soon, but if you can't I want to come there.

I need to finish this latest issue with Nova before I'm okay to travel. I have to at least be able to drive around outside without crying! Maybe I'll imagine you riding around with me.

Sunday, May 29

6:30 a.m.

excerpt from email to Bob

Good Morning!

And it is a good morning! I love it when life feels like a real treat.

It was so very hard to talk about, to take aim at an issue, to circle it and write a little about it before I would run for another direction.

That way truly lay dragons.

It is strange that all you have heard from me is all this hard, bad stuff. I really did have some good years in the last 30 some years! I haven't always been so dysfunctional. Part of this has been realizing that myself, but I don't know that you know it. Yet it is clear that you like me, so you must know that there is still more to me than what you hear.

I haven't written anything yet about how people think of me, as you suggested, but I am listening to what people are saying. And it's true; I've been dismissing them, especially in the program. I tell them I am doing some really rough therapy, and going some places that I haven't been before. That it is hard and scary. They say they really love me and I am wise and help them a lot, that they need to hear what I say and are glad I am in their lives. And this is just in the last week! Both in the meetings, and one-on-one after the meetings. I didn't really notice that I was treating them like the old fan club members. You are right: who am I to dismiss what they say?

When I read the positive thing to Nova, that I am clean, and good, and worthy of love, I laughed at the idea that it could possibly feel true to me. I still don't believe it, but I am [a] little closer to thinking it may possibly be true.

You do know what a help you are to me in this, don't you? The other day when I was so crazy was the first time I talked to Nova between sessions. The only one going through this with me is you, and you are so supportive and encouraging and sure that I am not going to just get lost there, but that I am going to come out. You help me believe it.

I do not know if we get to stay in each other's lives for a long time. I certainly hope so, but I know that is not a given. But it seems nothing short of a miracle to me that you came back into my life right now, at this particular time of all times that it could have been. You said you thought you exaggerated some in the song you wrote, "Estoy Aqui." I don't see any exaggeration at all. I am fighting for my life.

Monday, May 30

5:30 a.m.

excerpt from email to Bob

I remember that yesterday morning was good, but today is not good at all. I didn't want to wake up, and now that I have I just want to cry. I had worked very hard so I did not have to know what I know now, so I didn't have to feel so bad, and now I do. I wish that man had just left me alone. I am going to make it through until my [12-step] meeting at 8:00 this morning, and then I will try to get Nova. I can live through that much. Just took two of the pills that stop seizures; maybe they will help stop the thoughts and the pain and the tears.

Boy, my Uncle Jerry was a walk in the park compared to the way I feel about my grandfather and myself. I know he was a bad man, but I feel like I am bad too. I remember telling Nova that if I was a grown-up I could have understood what was happening, but I was not a grown-up. But I think I should have understood and should have stopped him but it would just be a mess.

If I can't get Nova, if things don't get better I will go to the hospital, because it hurts very bad. I will tell them I do not think I can let myself live, and they will keep me safe. I have to believe there is a way for it to be over. I can hold on for an hour until I talk to Nova.

I am the woman who blamed herself for years because a man I was dating set me up for a gang rape. Hey, I am good at blaming myself. That one is over, but there is enough of it left for me to build myself a long scenario. I think I will stop that; that I can stop. All the things that came after that were not my fault, those other bad things you already know about. They are no longer a part of the story. Jerry is not a part of the story. I can let that be true; it is just my mind working against me. It is my alcoholic mind that wants to drink playing around. I know what to do with that. I don't have to play there. Regardless of what God is to me at the moment, God will fight the desire to drink, and all the craziness that can lead me there.

This is firmer ground. I do not have to convince myself that my thoughts are wrong in order to not drink. I just have to know that the end result is wrong, and let God fight the alcohol. It is the same with killing myself. It is not good to link all of these things and think that my whole life has been full of men pulling at me and touching me all the time. It is also not true. I feel that when I stop and talk to you.

I bet you wish I was still just journaling and not dumping all this on you! I am sorry to bother you, and that in itself is sad. I cannot make myself go so far as to call Nova so early in the morning, but this will not wake you up and it is making me feel better.

I don't know if I could survive it getting worse! But it is moving around in my head now, to be just the time with the bad man instead of all of the other ones. Maybe I can just work with myself to box it up, and just put it in an empty room up there. Not behind the stone walls, easily accessible when it is time to unpack some more, but I can just not unpack any more right now.

So it is limited to the time with that bad man, and it is all packed up in a box and I will deal with it later. I will call Nova after my meeting. Maybe I will call her from the club [where the 12-step meetings are held] so if I cannot get her, I still will not be alone. That sounds like a way to make it through the next few hours.

They are all there, all boxed up neatly and ready to be unpacked when I want to unpack them. I do not have to do it now, I do not have to do it alone, I do not have to do all of this now. It has waited many years; it can wait a few hours more. But I hope you are right, and this is all of them! There has been enough drama and trauma for a lifetime. I don't want any more.

Unfreezing Trauma

My poor little girl! She is the one who is so broken up over this. She is the one who is screaming and crying and can't ask for help. I am the one comforting her as much as I can, and asking for help, again as much as I can. I may not be excellent at it, but we are still alive and have stopped crying now. Her feelings are in the box, and we will take care of them later, a little bit at a time.

She had a wall in front of her, and another wall behind her. Both walls are gone now, but the box is enough. It is temporary, and it will be sufficient.

I am not in as much pain now.

There are lots of activities going on today. Maybe I will see if Beth wants to go do something. She's a little worried about me; I gave her most of my drugs so there aren't enough in my house for me to do something stupid. That is a standard practice in recovery; if you have to take drugs, then let someone else dole them out to you. It's usually to prevent using them to get high, but it works to prevent overdosing to get out of pain as well. I hope she isn't working open to close, but she often does that on Mondays.

I'll think of another plan. I am leaving the boxes packed up and moving away from them today, right now, with you.

I could not make myself go out and work in the garden yesterday. I will not work in the garden as some kind of self-imposed punishment. The time will come when it will feel like a joy, and then I will do that. I know that time will come ...and in plenty of time for the food to grow and ripen.

I did go out with some friends for brunch yesterday, but then stayed in most of the day, reading, watching TV, and hiding out from feelings. Talked to several people on the phone for hours. It was okay until later at night, then it got bad.

But that was only part of the day. Part was good.

And the sun is shining now, and it is time to go to my meeting, and I made it through the early morning! Hooray!

I know this is not pleasant, and is not the most attractive aspect of myself to show you, but it is only truly out of my head when I send it on. So I'm going to.

I am taking care of myself, albeit in odd ways.

1:00 p.m.

excerpt from email to Bob

Just a short note, then it's time for a nap. I found Nova at her office, and we packed all the stuff up and put it in a foot locker and stuck it in the trunk of her car. I am not going to think about it except with her. I believe that I still don't know the whole story, that as I raged the other night, other things came out, and that there is still more that I don't know. I am not going to do that alone.

Meanwhile, I am thinking of wrecked cars and crowbars. That will be nice. Maybe by the time I've learned all about it, I will have found a car I can trash. Wham! There goes a window! Yeehaw!

I got *My Fair Lady* for this afternoon, and maybe a picnic with a bunch of recovering people, depending on how I feel after my nap and whether the rain that is threatening actually happens. I may take Anthonie [one of Phyllis' foster boys] with me. Beth is coming over after work; I found a Fred Astaire movie that neither one of us has seen, so we'll be watching that together tonight.

So I am okay, and will continue to be so.

Tuesday, May 31

6:30 a.m.

excerpt from email to Bob

We did some EMDR yesterday at Nova's office to put all the stuff away. It took several sets of the eye movements. I am so glad it worked! Though it works so well ... Think of the power. It is totally necessary for me; I don't think I could get through all this stuff without it. But it does give me the ability to really change things .... We all have these pivotal points, these remembered things that form us in some deep way. With EMDR, I can revisit those points in time and have a mind/emotion meeting and defuse them. It is an awesome power, when I think of it. Rather than spend years in therapy, and have the therapist define things in many ways for you, EMDR gets there quickly and you are in control. I hear Nova rooting for the positive that I have identified, but the rearranging to believe, that is all mine. It gives me more control over myself than I would have thought possible. Hard, yes, but amazing.

In the [12 step program's] fourth step and continuing through the seventh step, you attempt to identify your character defects, and ask to have them removed. An initial response to this idea is that if all our defects are removed, we will not know who we are! It is a scary thought to become someone else. I know that I have inside myself many beliefs that make absolutely no sense, that are illogical and that my mind does not believe. If I get to the point where my feelings and my mind are in sync ... it is mind-blowing for me. Do you find that you have many of those disconnects inside you? Where what you feel and think are so totally apart?

Or is this just me? I wonder as well about how many of us are interested in getting rid of those things.

Finding the balance, that is the key! This morning, I have a sense of peace. And a feeling of calm waiting. It's good.

2:00 p.m.

excerpt from email to Bob

For the other things, I was okay enough to handle the fallout on my own, but this one I need help with handling. And it is wonderful that the footlocker in the trunk is working.

The process is getting started in a major way; the last three months have been devoted to it. I now am at a point where I cannot handle the pace, where the problems really are too embedded and overwhelming for me to work on daily.

You wrote, "But now you're a strong, brave woman who can take what the strong, brave girl was unable to take."

Wow. And this is it, perfect timing. I was surprised when I read that, and in the last few days (you wrote this yesterday or the day before, I forget which) it has been a theme. It had to be my strong, brave woman who helped my little girl survive since Thursday, and who finally found a way to give her some relief from the unending pain and self-hatred in a way that let her know we would be finding the answer to that, that it would end, but that she could relax and be okay in the process.

And you named her for me. It is me being strong and brave! And the body that I inhabit now should show that! Got a ways to go, but it is true! That is what my body should be. The reflection of me, just as my picture of the little girl with the addition of her helmet and dust mop is who she is, and recognizable as such.

That is what my body should be! Not a disguise, not a way to hide, not a shell that protects me or an image that leads people astray. None of that. It can just be me.

I can work. I can do anything I want to do. I am not stopping in the process of learning from what has happened so far simply because I am not going on alone with the latest thing. Things are continuing to happen, and to be discovered.

I am stopping discussion of the bad man and all that entails, but the other things ... I am still learning from them, and hope to share them with you.

But my rate should be slowing down. I am not yet there; my little girl is totally overwhelmed with how bad she is, but she is believing Nova and you that she will get through this, and that it really is not true. She is trusting me to not take her there so fast that she wants to die or is hurt too much. She is trusting me with timing, and I will not fail her.

I had to build boxes to put so many other sexual experiences into so that the time with you was always a part of love, was always a spiritual encounter with the wonder of you. The system did not work well, but it was only a few weeks ago that you had such a time with me, explaining that the boxes were not real.

It seems very long ago. I know that I did not send you all of my journal entries. Did you get the one when I woke up one morning and realized that it could be a very silly-looking thing? It just felt odd that I did not always know that. Odd that we spent so many pages in conversation for me to realize that without negating the other aspects of sexual experiences.

I am the strong one, and I can stand what no one else can. That is no longer true. I am strong, but all of us are, and together we can get through things.

Wow. I believe that as I write it. There are people around me who can help, and you are one of them. There are some who cannot. It is a distinction that I can make, like who is a predator and who is not, like who is mean to me and who isn't at work.

I also spent some time this morning with an amazing woman who knows a lot about mental health. She brought up her little girl, who is the lost one for her. It was good to talk to someone else who is on somewhat of the same path at this moment!

Wednesday, June 1

4:00 p.m.

excerpt from email to Bob

It's not a very good day, but I'm okay. I realized that tomorrow was Thursday, and I really do not want to open all that shit up again. I've been comforting myself, saying I don't have to go there. Nova and I can just talk about it; we don't have to open it up. But then I get all worried about working, and not being able to do it when I'm working. If I can put it off until after the semester is over. Just worried about everything in general, I guess. Not much I'm not worried about at this point, except this month's bills. These ups and downs are a real drag; I was so up yesterday. Went and checked my email at work yesterday, whittled it down from 396 to 89 that I actually have to read. And felt fine doing it! Now, I'm worried about the fact that I haven't gotten anything from the college about semester start. So I'm worried about working, and worried about not working. I really can't blame it on anything but my attitude when I do that kind of thing!

It was a 10th-step meeting this morning, which means we were talking about all these defects of character and the space I was in — I was nothing but defects. A woman I've been working with called me, and I talked to her for about an hour. She has so many reasons why she drinks; it's not the alcohol but the ex-husband and the kids and the boyfriend and the job ... blah, blah, blah, making up reasons to drink. She finally said it was easy for me, since I had the perfect life.

And so I got loud and paced around the room and let her have a no-holds-barred version of my life that was anything but perfect. It's hard to go there, but I may have gotten through. It is simple -- don't pick up a drink. It is not necessarily easy.

Went out and worked the soil for a while, and hopefully will be putting my garden in. Except for the tomatoes, which I couldn't find at the nursery I went to.

And you, poor guy, you are just getting to hear me bemoan my fate! And lo and behold, I am feeling a little better. I'm just tired and out of sorts and worried. Been waiting to feel better to write you, and it hasn't happened.

So that is the story on this end. I feel sometimes like a wind-up toy that is hung up on something, just can't seem to get traction to do much.

6:00 p.m.

excerpt from email to Bob

No, I don't know that I am not full of defects! It's the black-white stuff. It's the little girl morality: there is no difference between stealing a nickel and stealing a million dollars, wrong is wrong. That is how I feel and if I could wave a magic wand and change it, I would. Me and Hitler are the same. I KNOW that is crazy, I know that the logic is all wrong, but it is how I feel and I don't know how to make it go away. I wish I did. None of me likes this; we just believe it. It makes me very sad.

I am doing the best I can today. It's not like I'm trying to do this. It's seepage, toxic seepage.

Thursday, June 2

5:30 a.m.

excerpt from email to Bob

I had absolutely no idea that all this emotion about my grandfather was stuffed somewhere in my mind. I wasn't conscious of it at all. I cannot seem to keep it boxed up very well, and it is incredibly powerful. When it is hitting me, it's is still overwhelming and extremely toxic. I hope Nova has some ideas tonight. This is a pivotal thing that happened to me and has affected my entire life in ways that I am only beginning to understand. It is so painful; the self-hate is so strong. I will ask Nova about the process of getting hospitalized; that seemed a possibility last night. The idea that I am too bad to live .... No wonder I had to hide this stuff when I was young! It's incredibly hard to deal with right now! I'm realizing that this one may take a long time, and I don't know how this can be done. On one hand I visualize all these sessions with Nova just to stop the seepage enough to work. That seems like such a waste of her time, and the exact opposite of what needs to happen.

But last night as I was finishing my garden after the heat let up, a very strange certainty that I should go in the house and take an overdose of what pills I had left (Beth still has most of them) came over me. I just kept playing with the dirt and watering until the thoughts went away. It felt like hours. I am not very stable from moment to moment. The days have been too wild this week.

My boss wants a note from some medical provider about my current condition; he mentioned this back when I took all the time off. I want to ask Nova to write one, and I don't know if I can work or not. I will not work if we can't get this suicide stuff put away. I am concerned about my state of mind. I have been able to deal with the storm so far, but this week has been hard. I am behind on shopping, haven't been cooking much, all my clothes are dirty, and my house is a mess. And no, sir, that is not the normal state of affairs here!

I'm working little by little on it. When I am engulfed by emotions, I don't get anything productive done, and I don't think it is that important. I just try gentle little "you are okay, we will be okay" messages to all the turmoil inside, and distract myself.

12:15 p.m.

excerpt from email to Bob

Wow. I've been on the go since 8:00 a.m. and just now got back home. If I was supposed to work today, I certainly could have! And I would have enjoyed it as well.

I seem to be telling a lot of people about this, the bare bones of being molested by my grandfather. It's like it can never be a secret again, because too many people know. It is just particular friends in the program, not my family. It is not all that uncommon from all the responses that I get. Many people took the route of busting the relative for it, and were put through hell by the rest of the family. Don't want to do that, could not stand getting blamed for it by others, or having my word doubted.

I really was thinking things were winding down and that I'd just keep getting better without all the backlash. But think how well hidden it was ... all the stuff I put you through about getting lost in sex was part of it, the earlier pains that my little girl went through protecting it, the detective part of looking for the rest of the thoughts that led to it. On my good days, it is just so exciting to think about it being resolved, about not feeling that way and how it will open my life up. It seems that way today.

If I had not gotten past the so-calm idea that I should go in the house and take all the drugs I could find, I would not have gone into the house. I would have gone to the Mental Health emergency center, part of where Nova works, and tell them I was suicidal and scared. They would have kept me. I need to find out more about the process, if I should use her name, that kind of thing. It's a precaution. This whole thing is really strong, and I want to live through it.

I did take a drug overdose to try to kill myself once, so I know that it is possible for me to go there. The calmness, the matter-of-fact way I was thinking about it last night was scary. And then it was over.

I have been remarkably free of seizures this week. No major ones at all. They may have found a new way to express themselves in the pain and the thoughts of suicide and drinking and getting laid and all the other negative impulses I've been dealing with.

That is actually a good thing. The seizures may stop once I get some more stuff processed.

6:00 p.m.

I tried to go back over the week and reconstruct it for the session. I pulled together the emails to Bob so I could use them to tell Nova what happened, and then used the emails to try to remember how I made it through the week. It was a very hard week to live through.

Besides now, I only wrote in the journal once after the last session, and it was because the process left me so upset and scared. I can hardly believe it as I write. Everything from last week except for that is just emails to Bob. I knew when I was talking to him the bad stuff did not come out. I could not face letting all the bad stuff find the keys, find the words to tell me things. It was hard enough to live through the week without all of that abuse from myself.

The session was last Thursday, a week ago. Friday was so bad I had to call Nova. Saturday, Bob called me and kept me from going insane. Sunday night was hard to live through. I wanted to drink, to find some good drugs, to get laid, to do something to stop the pain. By Monday, I wanted to kill myself and was afraid I would. I called Nova, and went to see her at her office to pack up the memories so I could get through the day. Tuesday was wonderful, but Wednesday was really bad. Wednesday early evening was when I was sitting on the swing, watering my garden, refusing to move until the calm notion of killing myself left.

Bob told me that Nova would have a plan, that together we could work it out, and I believed him. I am holding on to the belief that somehow it will be okay, that I will make it through tonight and this next session. I just need to sit here and not go anywhere and then Nova will be here. She will be here soon. And she will have a plan so it will be okay.

SESSION THIRTEEN

Friday, June 3

I read Nova the emails and spent some time telling her how crazy I felt. She thought it was good that I was telling people, and good that I had a plan on how to avoid suicide. But she didn't stay there long with me; she wanted to move on.

She told me that she had just talked to someone and found out that the EMDR could produce such changes in the brain that they showed up on an MRI. The week before, I had not done very well in watching the fingers move, and we would do it today with me watching her fingers.

She said that the memories from the week before were not like the ones we had done previously. As she talked, I was struck by the difference. The other things we had targeted were clear. The emotions may have been frozen, but I knew what they were, I knew what had happened, when Alex had beat me up, when Preacher had terrified me with talk of cutting off my head, when Walter's friends and relatives had gang-raped me. I knew all about them going into the session.

So this was going to be the session where I knew all about what happened with my grandfather, and I was going to watch her fingers and revisit it.

We used the same negative cognition [as in Session 12] with the addition of one line, "I should die." The week between had made me know that I thought I should die for this. The positive changed to add [the opposite of] the same thing. "I should live free and happy."

Start of the Session

Negative Cognition: I am dirty and bad and unclean and unworthy of love, and I should die. *Belief:* Near the top of the scale

Positive Cognition: I am clean and good and worthy of love, and I should live free and happy. *Belief:* Feels completely false

So we started. Some place, the living room at my grandfather's house. Same scenario, sitting on the couch with my grandfather. This time I followed her fingers. Rather than the horror at the actions, I was feeling the emotions. It was not such a big deal to me at the time. It was something that shouldn't be happening, or he wouldn't be sneaking. I had not been told to look out for this; I didn't understand what was going on. I was not aware of an incest taboo. The taboo was supposed to affect him, not me! I didn't know about it!

All I knew was the line from the examination of conscience, that said I should not touch the secret and sacred parts of my body, and should not see or touch the secret and sacred parts of someone else's body. So when he would go for contact there, I would run, fight, just get away. I knew that was wrong. I did not know that he shouldn't be touching me trying to arouse me and succeeding in doing so.

Nova talked about the incest rule being different in different places, and I suddenly realized we were in Kentucky. Kentucky! Where girls marry at 12, where incest seemed the rule rather than being taboo. I have a degree in anthropology, for goodness sake! Let's think about taboos! The biggest taboo there at that point was against interracial sex. Inter-family was the rule in the hills, and while it might have been less frequent in the big city, where my grandfather lived, it wasn't that big a deal. Not in that place, not in that time. Especially not in the time my grandfather had grown up.

I changed position; I even moved around the table at one point, with Nova working to maintain the eye movement on my part. I wouldn't notice when I would just move my head instead of my eyes, but she did and kept me on track. We went from place to place in his house, talking about his line of attack there. The basement shower – I think my sisters and I knew he would try to catch you there, and so there were always two of us, one to keep lookout from granddad. We knew he would try to see us naked, maybe we even knew he would try more if he caught us there alone.

The dining room, where he would stick money in my bra. Just to cop a quick feel. And I didn't feel like it was a guilty secret; I would tell my mother about the money, and she would tell me what

I could do with it, or if I should just give it to her. I just didn't mention how he had given it to me.

My mother warned me about the neighborhood boys, of the dangers of tackle football. Don't let those boys tackle you and put their hands all over you. But no warning of seductive men and slow touches that would make you crazy. I just did not know!

Nova and I went through it all. And when we went looking for where the guilt came from, we ran into St. Maria Goretti. She died rather than submit to a man touching her; she was stabbed to death and made a saint because she resisted.

End of Session

Negative Cognition: I am dirty and bad and unclean and unworthy of love, and I should die. Belief: the bottom of the scale

Positive Cognition: I am clean and good and worthy of love, and I should live free and happy. Belief: Feels completely true

I did not trust how okay I was feeling at that point. I wanted to clear this up more before Nova left. So I went and found the book *In Garments All Red* [the story of Maria Goretti]. It was stored in my trunk in the basement.

She was me -- 12 years old and oldest girl, taking care of the family and helping her mother; determined to be good. Her first Holy Communion was a mystical event for her, as mine was for me. We were the same.

Except she knew when the boy asked her to let him have her that this was wrong, that God did not want her to do that and that she had to resist with everything in her. He had approached her twice before and she had escaped. But she didn't tell her mother. Because she didn't want her mother to worry, she kept it to herself, like me.

How did she know? She knew earlier in the story that it was wrong to tell off-color jokes. She told her mom she'd rather die than do anything that bad. How did she know what they were about? She was 12 and it was around 1909.

I think they lied in the book! There were pictures and he was a handsome boy, maybe a little older than her. Maybe he was just courting her. Maybe he wanted to marry her.

Unfreezing Trauma

And he never even touched her secret parts! At the end, he had held her down with his knee and begged her to let him have her, and when she said no and he stabbed her. Fourteen times, not the 30-some I remembered.

I didn't know instinctively like she did that this protection from the evil and seduction of the world was worth dying for. I should have known and should have died — that is what it was all about!

How incredible. I don't believe that now, not for a minute. It was the church using parts of a story to make a point against bad books and magazines and movies, against the changing role of women.

I know we studied the book in St. Ann's, so it had to be when I was at the oldest 12 or 13. In Catholic school, one of the joys of my life was daily Mass. I had thought about becoming a nun. The nuns told me the story. We studied it in class and it was written by a priest so it was true.

They were wrong. A lay teacher could never have taught us that; she would have known different! But I believed them, and so I knew in my heart that I should be dead.

Nova said she had trouble understanding what I thought was so wrong the week before, when I kept saying I just sat there and didn't do anything. This explained it.

I see it now, and it amazes me, the layers I laid over it for years, the certainty in my heart that I should be dead, that I was bad. The need to be so very good, to work so hard, to try so hard, to be so hard on myself ... All of that came from this little book. This book and the lies it told, the lies they told me -- that was why I wanted to kill myself. The sheer enormity of my breach with God, the injunction against giving into the seductive ways of the flesh, had overwhelmed me.

My mind reels at the thought. On one hand, it is such a small thing. Just a book that we studied in school. It was not three or four years of fairly mild sexual abuse at the hands of my grandfather; it was the evil at the hands of the Church. It was God turning his back on me in disgust. It was missing the chance of a lifetime to become a martyr!

It seems ridiculous.

NOVA'S COMMENTS ON SESSION THIRTEEN

During the following week, it was almost as if the explosion of "the mother lode of rage" in Session 12 hadn't happened. All that remained of the insights in Session 12 was Mary's knowledge that (for some reason that she couldn't fathom) she should be dead. That is the way it should be. And she spent seven terrible days trying not to follow that clear injunction, to be dead, to kill herself. In Session 13, Mary revisited the experiences with her grandfather, and found out that she hadn't felt all the guilt and shame at the time, that his attempts at seduction had been almost pathetic, something she and her sisters recognized without exactly knowing, and avoided rather easily. So where did the death sentence originate? It was after the EMDR session that Mary remembered her book and brought it up from the basement. The story of Saint Maria (Mary) Goretti explained Session 12 and the dreadful week Mary had just managed to live through.

It all made perfect sense in the understanding of a good little Catholic girl. And because all the feelings were finally clear and understood, the grown-up Mary was free. "I don't believe that for a minute!" The power of the buried assumptions was immediately dissipated. It was a thrilling moment.

INTERVAL THIRTEEN

Friday, June 3

6:45 a.m.

I know at this moment that there is nothing wrong with me. I look forward to a life as a good, clean person, worthy of love. I don't feel that right now. It has changed since last night. I just feel sad that all my life I thought I should be dead and, that in the midst of falling in love, I had to work so hard to avoid knowing I should die. I was again giving into the evils of the world, but at that point it was hopeless. I was doomed. I was doomed with Bob.

Rather than going on being clean and happy, I am thinking how this warped my life and warped all my relationships. It certainly explains Tommy Walker, the necessity of dying was certainly a theme to our entire relationship. And to avoid that death we went to drugs and alcohol. When I finally broke with him, it was because I knew deep inside that one of us was going to have to die in that relationship and I did not want to die.

I think there is sadness to go through here.

9:35 a.m.

I just want to cry. I want the life back that I missed. I want the time back. I want to do it all over, knowing what I know now. I am aware of the fact that I cannot do that, that those times and places, those people and situations, are gone, are in the past. But I am so sorry that is true. I want to do it over again.

It is okay to be sad; it is not going to go to suicide and that is good to know. It explains why I felt it should all be different when I got married. Wouldn't I feel clean and worthy, like I was finally right with God?

It [sex within marriage] wasn't any different. The fact that I was so responsive, the fact that I felt such physical connections to people, that I longed to touch those I love — I could not cut that out of me. And as long as I felt that, I knew somewhere inside I needed to die.

I so long to be held and know that it is okay, that it is good, that I am not bad, that I do not deserve to die, that I am blessed to be able to experience joy with another person. But I think what I actually get to do is let the poison drain out of me minute by minute, hour by hour, until it is gone. I have to mourn all the people I have truly loved, what could have been and never was.

I don't think the Creative Power of the Universe, the power I can draw on and be part of, the power that allows me to be sober, wanted this to happen to me. I have to remember that things can get better, that I can find joy. But I am so sorry that I missed so many years, that I was warped.

I think last night cemented that I do not have to die, that I can live. The rest of the positive, that I am clean and good and worthy of love, doesn't resonate, just the sorrow. It is a process, I think. I am still getting better.

Saturday, June 4

6:00 a.m.

This is not like the other things I have dealt with, that I can touch with my mind and do a reading, think of something in particular and see what has changed. This is too big. Like Monet's Water Lilies at L'Orangerie. The rooms there are round, and all the walls are covered with the [one] painting. It was my dream to see this place. I sat at my teacher's station at the college before I went overseas and looked at pictures, imagining what it would be like. When I made it to Paris to see it, I had no response. Just none at all. It was too big; I was surrounded by it. I went twice in my four-day stay in Paris, but never did get a twinge of feeling. This was totally amazing. The first time I was in the actual presence of a Monet,[a smaller picture, not the giant room-sized water lilies] the beauty hit me like a bucket of water. It awakened me to a whole world of color and joy in the world.

It truly is a new world. It seems I move but a little in my head and I just don't know the place. I am scared and overwhelmed. I had slight seizures Thursday night, and harder seizures last night.

Nova sent me a wonderful letter and reminded me that now I can believe the people who think I am an exceptional woman.

Today I think about the future and cry. Is it really over? Can I really believe that? I remember when I first noticed I was not afraid to go outside, and it was wonderful. This, though, this is too much to notice all at once. Like a person coming out of years in a dark prison, kept there unjustly: the light is so strong and it is hard for the prisoner to believe it is true. Instead of dancing with joy and running in the sunshine, she stands, uncertain, just shading her eyes from the glare of light, stealing glances at the guards as if waiting for them to take her back.

I feel kind of like that.

I am okay. My little girl is subdued as well! Strange behavior from her.

I think I will work in my garden. It feels like half of my head is gone, the right half. All my thinking is going on in the left side, and it is strange. Like there has always been an echo from over there to thoughts over here.

Sunday, June 5

5:20 p.m.

I was so excited and high on life this morning that I called and sent emails to people telling them that I was exploding with joy. I felt as if the whole world was opening up to me, that I was part of the Cosmic Mind. Emailed Bob (excerpt below). Got to talk to both Bob and Rob, which was fun. Rob reminded me that breakthroughs are the fun part, that staying aware of what I was thinking and looking for is important.

excerpt from email to Bob

> I cannot believe how good I am feeling today! It is totally amazing. There is no resistance inside me to enjoying life. I want to have fun! I want to meet people, go places, do things ... sing and dance and

turn cartwheels for the sheer fun of it. It is so incredible! I may never get rid of the seizures, just like I will never stop being an alcoholic. Oh, well! It will still be a life full of joy! I am invited to enjoy life, and I think I will.

My day has been wonderful, and I've been doing all kinds of things. It feels strange, with half of my head feeling really empty, but there is a freedom in it. I don't think that side of my head doesn't work; I think it was REALLY bound up in all the secret stuff and death wish and all that. And after I wrote that, I had to leave the keyboard and run around for a while, giggling!

It is like all these things I was so sure of are gone, and there is nothing that has taken their place but a curiosity and a desire to follow where the cosmic consciousness leads me.

Monday, June 6

10:30 a.m.

I woke up in a very slow, mellow mood that has just gotten better as the day has progressed. I have noticed that I am asserting myself a little more, protecting my time.

My sponsor Cathy called and we got to talk for a while. I told her all about how ecstatic I was yesterday, and how happy I am today. I am the only one who has control of my time, and no one has the right to my time if I don't chose to let them have some time. She was glad for me.

The incredible high from yesterday morning is not back, but I am happy. It is so nice to be happy for no apparent reason! Instead of sad for no apparent reason. I love that life changes, and that I change.

Wednesday, June 8

7:50 a.m.

I went to work for the first time in three months yesterday. I was looking forward to going back and seeing the next set of students. I have been happy and full of energy since Sunday and wasn't expecting trouble.

When I got home from work I was really tired, and that continued all day, despite a long nap. I got up this morning late, having hit the snooze many times. I am starting to think and feel in old patterns. The thought of work fills me with dread.

Do I just hate my job? Is this a "normal" reaction to work? People on average seem to hate their jobs and have trouble going back after a vacation. I have rarely felt that way, mostly loving my work, or at least I thought I did, which may be the same thing. Am I just moody or manic-depressive, as I was once labeled? What is the problem? I do not want to attack myself looking for answers, but I do want to think about this.

11:40 a.m.

It struck me at the [12-step] meeting that it is a matter of focus more than anything else. The main thing I am doing now is getting better, in mind and spirit and emotions and body. Working is simply a way to get money to pay the bills. But I am annoyed at work, and was angry at Phyllis for nothing important, upset at someone else for not doing what they had agreed to do. I can let that go, focus on growth, on my main goal.

Thursday, June 9

3:50 p.m.

Last night the old "I'm worthless, I'm unlovable" stuff hit, and I tried not to follow it anywhere. Suicide came up, but did not seem at all attractive. Then I went to bed and woke up with a nightmare. All I remember from it is the right side of my head exploded with pain and blackness. That's what woke me.

At first I thought I'd just write it down and send it off, but then I thought about the books I've been reading. So I picked up the book *A Path with Heart,* read a while, did a little meditation on "May I be filled with loving kindness" and then read some of *The Cosmic Game* [the Grof book]. The idea came that a guy I was supposed to tutor didn't show up, Phyllis had cancelled something we had planned, and I didn't like my day being rearranged by these other people. Those things had knocked me off kilter, and it made sense that I followed old paths. I do not have to go there. I have to remember that.

I finally got back to sleep imagining myself enfolded in a heart of loving kindness.

I am feeling much better. I see Nova tomorrow and want to check out the EMDR book for suggestions on dealing with some of the emotional stuff. Between sessions I think I need to work not on finding out "why am I feeling like this?" but on changing how I am feeling with some guided meditation and reading. That worked well last night.

Friday, June 10

5:25 p.m.

I am trying to get my mind together for the session with Nova.

It seems to me at this moment the biggest thing missing is the monolithic thinking breakdown. I have just been noticing it a lot. It is there with people in the [12-step] program. But I noticed that it is not there with the people at work. It is there when I look at friends or anyone else who try to rearrange my schedule or take advantage of me.

You are either for me or against me. I want to be with people in recovery, at the same time I don't want to.

Thoughts of unworthiness come back regularly, but they are not as strong. If I watch for them and talk about them, I can just chose a different path.

I've been thinking about friendships. I certainly need some. It's the whole "worthy" thing that gets in there. I didn't realize it until I was talking to Bob about it, but it is what happens in my mind. I meet someone and I assume they won't be interested in me, so I don't try to pursue it. I just was not aware of that before. I've also realized that I know very little about being in love. I have never been there without having all this other stuff active in my mind, the constant murmur of the past battering me.

Another thing: I have always been involved in some way in helping other people; I don't remember ever not thinking this was important. What has changed for me this week is that I have recognized that I used to be obsessive about it. Before I went overseas, I was involved in many groups, and would have meetings and other things scheduled from 6 a.m. to 10 p.m. at night. It was not okay for me to just have fun. I noticed that first when Bob visited, but it is true all the time now, that it is okay to have fun.

I used to get angry and judgmental when I saw the college watering their grass. It was about their paying less for water than me, and other problems I see with the water company. Now it is just another problem of the modern world that needs work, and some groups are working on it. It doesn't have to be me!

I went and met Nova's daughter Kate and noticed afterwards that I felt really competent and self-assured. The whole "Who do you think you are?" background bitching at myself was gone!

That is so weird. It is these little things that I have been discovering this week, good things as well as destructive little habits that I have to watch. I don't know what this means for tonight's session. Maybe we'll just do the whole thing again, but leave the incident open. I don't think I need to worry about the grandfather thing anymore.

SESSION FOURTEEN

Saturday, June 11

In last night's session, we tried looking at the feeling of bad, unworthy, unlovable, and did not focus on an actual event at the start.

Start of Session
Negative Cognition: I am dirty and bad and unclean and unworthy of love. Belief: Middle of the scale

Positive Cognition: I am clean and good and worthy of love Belief: three-fourths of the way to the top of the scale

What came up after several times of trying the eye movements was me as a child, in the living room, feeling sad. I was tired. There were things I thought I should do, but I was tired. I knew that if I left it undone my mother would have more work, and I wanted to help her. But I was just too tired, and I felt bad and guilty because I could not work anymore.

I noticed this time that I was just a child, and so I needed more sleep than my mother. It was okay to go to bed when I was tired. Adults need less sleep, and I shouldn't feel bad because I go to bed first. I remembered a time I stayed up all night sorting my mother's button box. When I was finished, all the buttons that were the same were bundled up together.

I know now it was a pretty useless thing to do. The button box was used for missing buttons; for new projects new buttons were bought. So the sorting wasn't anything that would help. But I felt wonderful when I did that. It was a good thing, I thought, to stay up all night working. It is one of the few times I remember doing enough.

End of Session
Negative Cognition: I am dirty and bad and unclean and unworthy of love. Belief: do not believe it

Positive Cognition: I am clean and good and worthy of love. Belief: almost at the top

Nova mentioned rescuing my mother. I wonder if it is rescuing. Is that what it is when I feel bad that my mother had to work so much? It isn't something that I feel about other people. I can't think of anyone right now that I think works too much. I knew that all my mother's work was stuff that needed doing.

Nova and I talked about taking a break. I rarely think I deserve a break; if there is work to be done, I should do it. I had to admit I believed that. Other people should take breaks. Other people need breaks. But it doesn't matter what I need. Someone has to do the work, and I feel that someone should be me. I am beginning to realize that is not right.

I am okay with sleeping when I am tired, or even just taking a break when I am tired. But sometimes I don't think I can give myself that option. Cigarettes allow me to take a break. Smoking gives me something to do that I have to do, and I feel justified in taking a break for a cigarette.

I thought about that when I saw a commercial for candy. People are in awkward situations and don't know what to do, so they stuff candy into their mouths. It gives them a break. They can't just take a moment to think, but have to justify taking that moment.

As we talked about old habits coming back through the week, Nova talked about a method called DBT [dialectical behavioral therapy, a type of cognitive behavioral therapy]. She will get me more on this, but the thing she wants me to try this coming week is this: when I feel old emotions, negative emotions, do the opposite action. When I feel like I should work and don't want to, instead of trying to figure out why I don't, I do something fun. I move my body instead of playing in my head with the emotion. That is a way to acknowledge the emotions but not go with it. I am going to try that. Thinking more about the negative and trying to understand it takes me farther into it.

NOVA'S COMMENTS ON SESSION FOURTEEN

This session felt like "real life." We can't shuck off our old skins and suddenly become brand new. Mary had finally understood the hidden assumptions that had been torturing her. But she still had to mourn the lost time, the years that she had spent wasting half her strength just carrying the burden. And she had to break old habits of thought, find out how to stay with the new perceptions. She said, "I feel as if half my head is gone!" Earlier, she had made a comparison with an alcoholic who comes into the 12-step program, hears "We need to get rid of our character defects" and wonders, "What will be left of me?" She had to make a whole new mental landscape without the powerful outline she had lived with since 12 years old.

INTERVAL FOURTEEN

Saturday, June 11

7:00 a.m.

I am okay with what we did last night. As I looked at last week, I noticed the self-abuse would start at night because I was not doing anything. It is now okay for me to rest at night, to say that whatever I have done in that day is enough. I don't think Nova knows what a big thing this is to me, to stop this night list of things not done.

I feel relieved when 5:00 p.m. comes, because I have convinced myself that I do not need to berate myself for phone calls not made after that. It is useless, since offices are closed.

9:00 a.m.

I did do well last night after Nova left. There were things I could have done last night, but I did not do them. I just read and watched TV. And consciously told myself that it was okay to do that — and believed myself!

As I think of it now, I wonder why I work more than other people. It's how I get promoted so much when I have a job (current job excepted). That may be something we should look at another time. But it [this idea that I need to work more than anyone else] is not as fiercely held as I have held it in the past; I am beginning to believe deep in my heart that I am allowed to play and it is okay to do things just for fun. That just came now; last night we did not go there.

Sunday, June 12

12:30 p.m.

I have been talking to Bob about getting this is in shape to be published. I really want everyone who has had some kind of trauma to know about this incredible method of relief. But it is hard, and I am sad after working through the first session. I really have done a lot of work, and changed in a lot of ways. I have to keep myself safe, though, and not do too much. I am writing this just to tell myself that I have to be done with it today, that I cannot do anymore.

I skipped my morning [12-step] meeting and did not feel bad about it. I got up late and did not have time to take a shower and get ready for the meeting. I am usually frantic to get to meetings, but it just didn't feel like I needed it today. I am less dependent on the meetings than I was just a week ago. I am getting better.

Tuesday, June 14

5:40 p.m.

It has been a pretty good day! I went to work. The new [instructional] program was up and running and I played with it with the other teachers, trying to figure out how to do things. I was excited about it. And at some point I just felt really good, happy, and excited, like I wanted to dance and laugh. Me, the woman who agonized over every minute at work just three months ago! Who hid out and just hoped she could make it through without a seizure or without screaming at someone.

I begin to think it was me, not them! How is that for an understatement? I really do love teaching math. And so do many of the teachers here, which is why I like them.

I sat down to write this because I haven't written for a while, and I just had another one of those "It's wonderful to be alive and I am happy" moments for no reason at all. I went out to mow the grass and it started raining. I spliced some wires on the speakers and hooked them up to the computer and they didn't work. So I just sat down and started reading a book and felt wonderful.

Who would've thought! It has nothing to do with whether things go my way or not. How amazing!

I am really enjoying turning this journal into a book. I guess I think the big stuff is over! But I am noticing things as I work through it, noticing how things have moved into memory, how the past is really the past in a new way. I noticed how wonderful it was that my little girl appeared when she did! In the morning I'm telling Bob that I am leery of moving on to the Preacher incident when the Alex incident is still so fresh. In the evening we don't go to Preacher at all, but to my little girl, and I find what Nova called my "core of strength." I hardly needed a safe place after that, since I had my little girl to be strong. And when she needed some strength, my big girl could help her.

But I can't stop doing everything else and just work on that. I have to strive for the balance. I have to keep reminding myself of that! I've finished [revising] through the fourth session, first time through. I know I will go back to it several more times, once with Nova, probably with Bob as well, before I try to get an agent to work with me on getting it published.

If it is still raining out there, I think I will just take an umbrella and go for a walk anyway.

Wednesday, June 15

10:50 p.m.

It was an incredible day. I did so many things. Went to a [12-step] meeting, mowed and trimmed the front yard, went swimming with Anthonie, Phyllis's foster child. Went to dinner with an old friend who is doing legislative advocacy. It felt so good to be full of energy!

I am getting better all the time. I feel so free, like it was all so very long ago. But it is less than two weeks since the "I should be dead, I should have died, I was stupid" stuff came out. Less than two weeks. Amazing.

When I was talking to my old friend about it, I was just laughing and enjoying that it was gone. It felt so wonderful to be out at night, and it is so good to not be afraid anymore.

It is incredible reading the journal, I make a blanket statement – I never feel this way, for example. Two lines later, I detail the time I felt that way. The monolithic thinking, everything black or white, always or never. And I don't notice myself saying that!

Thursday, June 16

5:30 p.m.

Nova will be here soon. I just wanted to get down the thought I had on the way home from work. I was thinking about groups.

I want to start a group called the Warrior Women. We can just hang out together when we can. Nova is one, and my sponsor Cathy. My old friend who is doing such good legislative advocacy. And the amazing teacher with MS from work. And me! Women who have overcome serious problems and triumphed.

I like that thought and want to keep it.

SESSION FIFTEEN

Friday, June 17

Nova and I are winding down and coming to the end. We didn't do any EMDR, and it felt like there was nothing left to do! We are going to continue to see each other. I will continue to talk to her about the revelations in my life, about the things I notice in this totally new journey. I will continue to journal, but it is not going to be the same.

We spent most of the time just talking about all the wonderful things that are happening in my life. I look at what my life had become, and I am amazed as I watch myself go through a day. It is not just that the resistance is gone; it is that spontaneity and joy are back.

I like my job! What a surprise that is. I can do things in the world! My world was so small, so limited. It is open now — and I like that!

NOVA'S COMMENTS ON SESSION FIFTEEN

How pleasant it was to see and hear Mary so full of joy. It is hard for me, as it is for her, to realize that the week when she felt that she was "supposed to" be dead was only two weeks ago, two sessions ago. It has been an interesting journey, often with the answers preceding the question. Tonight Mary said, "I make a blanket statement that 'I never feel this way,' and two lines later I detail when I felt that way!" Earlier, in the interval before this session, Mary commented, "I don't know why I think I am supposed to work harder than anyone else." Several chapters earlier she explained how fervently she wanted to work harder than her mother, to be her best helper, to see her mother able to rest "because of me!" Today Mary was able to look at her behavior from an adult position, and free herself from a compulsion that stemmed from goals held by "little Mary." I think the two Marys are alike in their energy and desire to "do good." But "little Mary" wasn't burdened by the conclusions of her adult self. It is wonderful that adult Mary can choose her behaviors without being bossed around by her "little warrior."

INTERVAL FIFTEEN

Friday, June 17

8:00 a.m.

I have started rereading the journals. I continue to amaze myself. It is fascinating to me. I reread the wild part of May 3, when all my sexual activities merged and I fell apart. I realized I had never sent it to Bob and knew I had to do that. It still makes me cry, and I know exactly where I was at that moment. It was very brave to go on, but at the time, it felt like I was holding a live wire and did not know how to let go, did not know how to stop typing, and kept on until the death thing came out. Which I still didn't consciously notice.

The interesting thing is at the very end of that entry: I talk about how the thought that I should live is just something I made up. Long before it actually came out, it appeared for a brief moment, then hid again.

11:30 a.m.

I sent the May 3 journal entry that had the image of Bob kicking me to him. At this moment, as I think of the thing that horrified me the most from the May 3 journal, it was that image of Bob. It was only when I let the image actually come to me that I saw it, that I recognized it. I read the part about kicking, and it was the incident with Alex that came. I was on the floor by the couch, trying to protect myself from his kicks.

Bob morphing into Alex was about pain, I think. The most physical pain I experienced in any of these things was when I was down on the floor and Alex was kicking me. I can still see it and feel it. I need to do some more EMDR on this! For it is not totally over. I can still feel it. When I go there, it is not over; it is alive.

9:00 pm

I just got back from Anthonie's first ball game. There is something I really like about young people playing baseball; they are still doing amazing things. Three errors on one hit — it went past one guy, then another, then a third player missed the ball. Then they turned around later for a great double play. We had a moment there where there were two runners on third base. What can you do but laugh and shake your head? And cheer for them. I must admit, I have a hard time not always rooting for the batter!

It was another one of my "I can do it" moments. I was sitting here being weird. So when Phyllis came by and said she was going to stop by the game, I went and stayed 'til the end. I like to make loud noises.

My choice was to sit here and worry about nothing or go to the game. I went to the game. I didn't stop to think what do I have to do the next day, do I have enough energy for this — none of that stuff. I grabbed my purse and went. I am getting so much better!

And I bet I could have actually gone dancing tonight, after the game. I need to find some folks to dance with at a moment's notice! I'm not quite brave enough to go on my own ... yet.

The whole "am I worth it?" thing is being settled. I am worth good treatment! I am as worthy as anyone else. I am not less than, I am not bad, I am not stupid. I am as good as anyone else, and I deserve to be well treated.

"I am a child of the universe, no less than the trees and the grass, I have a right to be here." And to enjoy being here.

I just feel like that.

Thursday, June 23

5:00 p.m.

Life is good. There is a joy inside me that bubbles calmly or bursts out, but it does not leave. My life is back, and I am anxious to enjoy it. I am so active.

This morning at the meeting I met a Vietnam vet who has horrible nightmares. He is on lots of medication, which controls his dreams most of the time. And when they come, he has a mantra -- it is over, it is not real. I told him when that was no longer enough he should try EMDR, where frozen memories become actual memories.

    I am turning the journal into a book for him and everyone like him. I am no longer worried about the world knowing my story, about my father being hurt, about my family turning against me and defending my uncle. I am not going to apologize for my vision of the world. It is as valid as anyone else's.

SESSION SIXTEEN

Friday, June 24

Last night Nova and I looked once again at the couch from the first session. I read what I had written since the last session, about Bob morphing into Alex, and then read some more. We went back to May 3, and reread the diatribe against men, against Bob, against myself.

Then I watched her fingers and went back to the time with Alex. No cognitions, nothing but an attempt to look and see what had happened, what I had missed. Why was it still alive?

It was the same as before. He came home in a cab, and wanted me to pay. I didn't have any money. He got angry. I was surprised at his anger; I was surprised when what I thought of as an argument getting a little physical turned into his doing serious harm. He knocked me to the ground, and I stayed there.

All I could see was the corner of the couch. All I felt was the growing pain in my stomach as he kicked and kicked. I didn't think he would stop; it just kept on.

I had started out being indignant. But now I was beaten, now there was no fight left, now I begged, pleaded, please stop. And he did. That was the moment I had missed before. He stopped, and for a brief moment it was over. I was okay. He was finished.

And then he started again with the verbal abuse, and talking about going upstairs. Even before he touched me again, it was the horror at knowing that it was not over. That was the moment, the pain, the betrayal, the cruelly false hope. They use this in horror movies, the moment of apparent safety, followed by an attack even more fearsome. It is powerful.

I went through that and recognized it. It was the same feeling I had later that evening when I had made it to apparent safety in my neighbor's house. Then Alex came in with his calm manner, and the neighbor woman tried to pry my fingers off the post. I had to relive the moment again.

I went through the false hope, and the rest of what I knew came back to be applied once again. It may not have ended then, but it did end. It was a minor setback on the way to being safe, but I ended up being safe.

How strange that it hadn't been defused. But it was defused now and could slip into memory. And then a whole chunk fell into place. The time line. I grabbed some paper, and started blocking out time.

Ora B and I were together about nine months, according to Phyllis. If that was correct, and it felt right, then I lived with her and the girls in that house for about six months. The gang rape Walter set me up for was when we moved in there, November 1975. I got pregnant with Jon near the time of the hostage situation with Preacher, in May of 1976. The beating by Alex happened between those two. It all happened in six months.

In my mind it had been so much longer.

I graduated from college with my first degree in June, 1972. I started work at a youth services program almost right away. I left there in 1974, late in the year; I couldn't work and drink at the same time. The descent into the hell of alcoholism had been so very swift. My mind is busy rearranging things as I write this, assigning different priorities and values. "What have I done with my life?" is becoming mostly good things, not bad. I spent only comparative moments lost in the darkness.

We did not do any more EMDR last night, but we talked a lot, read a lot, and made some connections.

We looked yet again at May 3.

We did not reread the incredibly long email exchange between Bob and me that finally convinced me he was correct in believing sexual activity is basically the same activity with a wide range of spiritual and emotional content.

The part we looked at was this part of where I felt the keyboard had me prisoner and I was just emptying myself into it, like a person who is caught in electricity.

> I don't want to talk to Bob about it anymore. I
> don't want to talk to anyone about it anymore. I just

know that I never want to go there again, I never want to get lost in sex again by myself, with only my stupid little head and stupid little fucking dreams. It's amazing that I am still fucking alive. Jack off, you bastards. Seems the only thing I add to that is a softer mother-fucking spot for the activity, and less wear and tear on the hand. How could I even have said as much as I did to Bob? Here's my little vulnerable neck, feel like kicking it? Cutting it? Stomping on it? Or just playing with it and messing my head up?

Son of a bitch! And my first response, my first fucking response to him is to try to make *him* not feel bad! Oh, thank you for destroying me, thank you very much. Did you hurt your boot when you stomped on my stomach? Sorry for being under your feet, sir! Why is *he* so fucking important that if *he* doesn't believe in it that it never happened?

We talked about the point where Bob seemed to turn into Alex. It was incredibly painful for me to give up my belief that being in love and getting lost together in that love was totally different from other sexual activities. It was the depth of pain that brought the Alex image in.

And it was only Bob who could destroy that, who could convince me. For he really was the one I believed in totally. Our love was wonderful. Love could be wonderful and good, and the physical expression of that love was magical. No matter what else happened, at the core of my being sat Bob, steady as a rock, holding out the promise of being loved.

And more than that. The ending of the diatribe, the point where I finally could stop typing that horrible night. We read again the last part.

> I want to stop this but it just keeps going on. I am so sad. I am so tired. There's nowhere really to escape. Come on, get a grip here. All you have to do is stop this. Stop typing; then none of that stuff will come at you from the keys or from your head or

from wherever it comes from. Oh, Nova, is this just another thing I can go through? The last bit in my head that is there to hurt me? Can it just be that?

And there I go, making things up again. I just make things up. Think of a rope to Nova; hold on to the rope and you will be okay. But that is not real; I just made that up. Like my fantasy of love that I just made up. Like my fantasy of community that I just made up. Like I should live, which I just made up. Like anyone really cares.

"Like I should live, which I just made up." It was about deserving to live. I fought so incredibly hard to not believe what Bob had said because it was the basis of my belief that I was worthy of life.

I was 12 when the knowledge that I should be dead entered my soul. It never left until a few short weeks ago. I rejoice in its absence every day. But why was I still alive?

Nova asked that, and I laughed. "Because I was so bad at suicide!" I told her.

It all makes sense to me. I buried the knowledge that I should be dead, covered it for years with concrete and walls, fought against it. At its core was sexual activity, giving in to the pleasures of the flesh, losing my only chance at martyrdom, at total connection with God, by allowing my grandfather to arouse me rather than be killed.

Then came the loss of my virginity, my first sexual experience, with a man who was unlike any I had ever imagined could exist. And he and how he made me feel became the opposing force to that knowledge that I should be dead.

I never forgot him. After we were no longer together, it must have been almost immediately, I made my first attempt to kill myself. Jumping in front of speeding cars, trying again and again until the police came for me. Then came the pill overdoses a year or two later, a vision of lying calmly on the bed, arms folded across my chest, drifting away to never come back.

The reality was I was conscious when death came to call. I felt the most intense pain in my life. I slipped into that unending darkness, and with all the strength I had I screamed on my way down. That scream alerted others and caused them to seek help for me. My next conscious thought was coming to in the emergency room to hear the nurses talking.

"These hippies and their drug use. Why do we even have to deal with them? We have people who are really hurt; we don't have time for this."

I slipped away again, into rest this time.

I was not brave enough or skilled enough for a gun. Nova mentioned a woman she knows who shot her shoulder trying to kill herself. That way didn't work very well. Hanging seemed to be pretty difficult as well. Slitting your wrists in the bathtub looked promising, sounded possible and maybe pain-free, but it didn't seem to work so well. Lots of people are running around with scars on their wrists.

So I chose alcohol, that pretend death, that absence of feeling that comes with blackouts.

I don't understand people who live with the knowledge that they cannot control their drinking. For a short while I believed I could control it, though I am still getting used to the fact that it wasn't a million years. As soon as I knew, in my heart of hearts, that I was powerless over alcohol, I knew the choice was to do whatever they told me in the 12-step program or kill myself. I chose the 12 steps.

I worked non-stop on recovery, doing the steps, as well as working in the recovery community relentlessly, for 27 years. The idea that I should be dead did not go away, though I was usually not conscious of it. But I was in full flight from it.

The core of the flight, the little hidden belief that I should be alive and happy, that it was possible to be alive and happy, came from the sunlit time with Bob. That is why I could not function during the week after I lost that and before I found and faced the death belief. I had no opposing force anymore. He had left me. He had told me that he was not there with me, that I had been alone in that place that did not have anything to do with sex [per se]and everything to do with love and joy and life.

Now my life can go on. Love and joy and laughter exist. I know that now. I know they are bigger than the tiny core where Bob and

I used to live. I am connected with a universe that is full of people and feelings, good and bad, in everchanging mixtures. I am alive.

EMDR RESOURCES

Find an EMDR clinician
www.psychologytoday.com Site for clinicians around the world, allows choice of area and choice of type of therapy, which includes EMDR. Up to date list, all listed are currently practicing.

www.emdr.com The site for the EMDR Institute, Listing includes all those who have taken EMDR training in the States. Lists includes some no longer in practice.

www.emdria.org more up-to-date than at emdr.com, but many practitioners are not listed

EMDR Training
www.emdr.com
www.emdria.com
www.emdrhap.org

Books I Found Helpful
EMDR: The Breakthrough "Eye Movement" Therapy for Overcoming Anxiety, Stress, and Trauma by Francine Shapiro and Margot Silk Forrest Basic Books, 1997

Emotional Hearing at Warp Speed: The Power of EMDR by David Grand Crown Publishing Group, 2001

Extending EMDR: A Casebook of Innovative Applications by Philip Manfield, W.W. Norton and Co., 1998

Peaceful Heart: A Woman's Journey of Healing by Aimee Jo Martin, Creative Arts Book Co., 2003 Available at ABE books online and other used bookstores.

EMDR Support Group

Facebook EMDR support group A group of therapists and those who have used, want to use, or are currently using EMDR in their lives who all share knowledge and experience.

OTHER RESOURCES

Alcoholics Anonymous (AA) www.aa.org General info and local contacts. The twelve-step group that started them all.

National Alliance on Mental Illness (NAMI) www.nami.org General information, local contacts, also has a help line 1-800-950-NAMI answered M-F 10 am – 6 pm

National Child Traumatic Stress Network (NCTSN) www.NCTSN.org Lists a wide variety of crisis lines on child sexual abuse, suicide prevention, etc. as well as information and resource pages and papers on a wide variety of child traumatic stress situations including school shootings.

National Domestic Violence Hotline www.thehotline.org 24 hour hotline at 1-800-799-7233 available 24/7/365 Website includes chat line as well as other resources and information for survivors who are currently in abusive relationships as well as those who have already left the relationship.

Rape, Abuse, and Incest National Network (RAINN) www.rainn.org Hotline answered 24/7 1-800-656-HOPE (4673) and live chat through their website. Survivors can find local resources using their zip codes and the hotline will redirect to local sources of longer term support as well.

Made in the USA
Monee, IL
18 July 2020